Ancient Secrets Revealed!

Sun Tzu wrote **The Art of War** over 2,500 years ago. The text has been treasured, preserved, and passed down through the centuries. However, until now, only a small number of Sun Tzu's ideas were understandable to the average reader. Now, for the first time, Sun Tzu's competitive system is explained in detail **in simple words and diagrams**.

This book contains **the complete text** of Sun Tzu's **The Art of War** in the most accurate translation available. It also contains a detailed, phrase-by-phrase explanation of Sun Tzu's text in words and pictures that allow you to put his powerful competitive methods to work.

This Book is only the beginning...

This book contains **the secret password keys** that allow you to access the Clearbridge Owners' Training Site (see **www.clearbridge.com** for information). This site contains hundred of pages of FREE training material to help you master Sun Tzu's techniques. You can download slide shows, study guides, e-books, screen savers, posters, and more.

Buy this book today and study its ideas forever!

Ancient Wisdom for the Future

Other *Art of War* Books
from Clearbridge Publishing

The Art of War: In Sun Tzu's Own Words
ISBN 1929194005
The Art of War & The Art of Sales
ISBN 1929194013
The Art of War & The Art of Marketing
ISBN 1929194021
The Art of War & The Art of Management
ISBN 1929194056
The Warrior Class: 306 Competitive Lessons
from Sun Tzu's The Art of War
ISBN 1929194099

To Mickie Wilson,
the most amazing mother-in-law on the planet.

AMAZING SECRETS

OF SUN TZU'S
THE ART OF WAR

BY
SUN TZU
&
GARY GAGLIARDI

CLEARBRIDGE PUBLISHING

Published by
Clearbridge Publishing

FIRST EDITION
Copyright 2001 © Gary Gagliardi

Manufactured in the United States of America
Front Cover Art by Gary Gagliardi
Back Cover photograph by Rebecca Wilson

Library of Congress Catalog Card Number: 2001090321

ISBN 1-929194-07-2
Clearbridge Publishing books may be purchased for business, for any promotional use, or for special sales. Please contact:

Clearbridge PUBLISHING
PO Box 33772, Shoreline, WA 98133
Phone: (206)-533-9357 Fax: (206)-546-9756
www.clearbridge.com
info@clearbridge.com

CONTENTS

The Discovery: SUN TZU'S SYSTEM IN DIAGRAMS ix

1. PLANNING 2
   AMAZING SECRETS OF COMPETITIVE ANALYSIS 3
2. GOING TO WAR 12
   AMAZING SECRETS OF COMPETITIVE ECONOMICS 13
3. PLANNING AN ATTACK 20
   AMAZING SECRETS OF UNITY AND FOCUS 21
4. POSITIONING 28
   AMAZING SECRETS OF AWAITING OPPORTUNITIES 29
5. MOMENTUM 36
   AMAZING SECRETS OF INNOVATION 37
6. WEAKNESS AND STRENGTH 44
   AMAZING SECRETS OF COMPETITIVE RELATIVITY 45
7. ARMED CONFLICT 56
   AMAZING SECRETS OF DIRECT CONFRONTATION 57
8. ADAPTABILITY 66
   AMAZING SECRETS OF OPPORTUNISM 67
9. ARMED MARCH 72
   AMAZING SECRETS OF COMPETITIVE EXPLORATION 73
10. FIELD POSITION 88
   AMAZING SECRETS OF EVALUATING OPPORTUNITIES 89
11. TYPES OF TERRAIN 102
   AMAZING SECRETS OF CAMPAIGN STAGES 103
12. ATTACKING WITH FIRE 124
   AMAZING SECRETS OF USING THE ENVIRONMENT 125
13. USING SPIES 132
   AMAZING SECRETS OF USING INFORMATION 133

This book was taken from
Gary Gagliardi's
live presentation,
THE AMAZING SECRETS OF SUN TZU'S
THE ART OF WAR

**For information about presentations
for your company or organization:**
Contact Clearbridge Publishing
206-533-9357
info@clearbridge.com
www.clearbridge.com

The Discovery: Sun Tzu's System in Diagrams

Sun Tzu developed the most complete and powerful competitive system of all time, but until now, those concepts were difficult to understand and utilize. He did not intend his methods to be used only in military confrontations as envisioned in the fifth century BC. He assumed that material and technology would change but that competition itself would always remain the same. He abstracted the basic, timeless elements of competition so that they apply equally well to any strategic confrontation in any era.

His book, *The Art of War*, was written at a high level of abstraction. Sun Tzu didn't write it as a training tool to educate the uninitiated. In his time, people learned the basic concepts of a school of thought directly from a living master. Books were supplements. They were designed for study after the basic concepts, metaphors and analogies were understood. Because of this, the text of *The Art of War* is extremely difficult for the average reader to understand. The purpose of this book is to address that problem.

After writing five other books on Sun Tzu's *The Art of War*, including a new translation from the original Chinese, I began diagramming his ideas for the slide shows I use in my live presentations on Sun Tzu's competitive methods. (These slide shows are available to our readers on our website: www.clearbridge.com.)

These diagrams act as the backbone for this book. In developing them, I discovered a previously unknown, geometric side of Sun Tzu's concepts. Much of the hidden detail and sophistication of Sun Tzu's system, especially in the interrelationship among its components, becomes clear when drawing them instead of trying to describe them in words alone.

Did Sun Tzu teach from diagrams like these and plan them as part of his book? We will never know, but, after developing these diagrams, I discovered that Chinese tradition used similar diagrams (the Bagua, the Flying-Star, the Element Star-Pentagram) in using the I Ching, Feng Shui, and Chinese astrology. These systems all predate Sun Tzu. They make it increasingly likely that, in constructing these diagrams from the text, we are actually seeing tools similar to those that Sun Tzu used in his time. These diagrams are truly an "amazing secret" hidden in the book.

My first discovery was what I called "The Eye of Sun." This simple diagram shows the interrelationship of the Five Key Elements that define competitive systems as Sun Tzu described in chapter one. The diagram that I came up with looks like this:

The Five Element Model
A picture of Sun Tzu's competitive world.

This diagram shows three layers: the competitive environment on the outside, the competitive unit, and the core philosophy.

The competitive environment is a unique feature of Sun Tzu's system. The environment defines the time and place at which competition takes place. Sun Tzu describes the time as *weather* and the place as *ground*. The ground is both where we fight and the *territory* we fight over. Weather (also known as *heaven*) represents time and change in general, but more specifically the *trends* that change over time. These elements are described in great detail in chapter one and throughout the book.

The next layer is the competitive unit or organization that is fighting for survival. In the diagram, the diamond shape is determined by the competitive unit's relationship with its environment. It occupies a specific position on the ground and under heaven. It is divided into two components as well. The *leader* is the person who heads the competitive organization and makes *decisions*. *Methods* are the techniques of the organization. Leadership is the realm of individual decision. Methods are the realm of group action.

Complex Concepts in Model
Elements have many aspects and meanings.

The core of the competitive unit is the *way* or the *philosophy* around which the group is organized. In business, we call this our company *mission* or goals. This core philosophy provides the group with unity and focus. It holds the competitive unit together, binding its people with their shared goal.

This Five Element Model became the basis of our system for explaining Sun Tzu's methods. The shape of the components helps define the characteristics that Sun Tzu attributes to them.

After developing this diagram, the *four skills* that the book describes fit easily into it. This view captured many of the complex relationships defining the skills. The skills of a leader are *knowing* and *vision*. Knowing comes from understanding our ground.

Model with Four Skills

Vision comes from studying the ground and heaven (trends over time). Method skills are *action* and *positioning*. Action, which results in keeping or changing ground, comes from having the right vision and good timing (Heaven). Positioning, which is the skill of using the ground, is the result of successful action and picking the place. Each skill cycle gives rise to another.

The four skills are never mentioned together because, in Chinese culture, four is considered unlucky. The word "four" sounds like the word "death." These skills are either addressed individually, or three skills are referenced together. In the later references, two skills are combined to make up the third. Knowing is usually combined with vision as planning. Action is usually combined with positioning as execution.

The four skills are also frequently referenced through metaphors. Knowing comes from listening, and it is always referred to as a sound. Thunder, music, and drums are all metaphors for knowledge. Keeping quiet is protecting knowledge. The metaphors for vision are sight, color, lightning, and so on. The metaphors for action are marching, moving, and, generally, "foot" work. The Chinese character for "act" is a pictogram of a foot. The metaphors for positioning are gathering food, building, eating, digging, and, generally, "hand" work.

After diagramming the skills, I added the five main types of attack: deception, battle, surprise, siege, and divide. There is a *sixth* type of attack, what I call, *environmental* attacks. The entire point of this final type of attack is that it falls outside of normal competition. Therefore, it falls outside of this diagram.

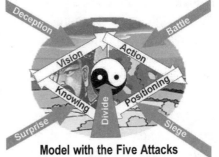

Model with the Five Attacks

As the above diagram shows, four of the main types of attacks are aimed at an opponent's skill. Deception is an attack on an opponent's vision. Battle is aimed at disabling actions. Siege is aimed at positions. Surprise is aimed at knowing. Divide targets the philosophy that holds the organization together. In many ways, this diagram defines the nature of these attacks better than the terms that we use, which only approximate the concepts that Sun Tzu developed in his work.

After I discovered this basic diagram, I found that Sun Tzu's other complex concepts become much easier to understand when they, too, are diagramed. This is particularly true of his three-dimensional model for evaluating opportunities and the nine-stage model he uses to define the situations that occur in a competitive campaign. We will introduce you to these models at the appropriate place as we go through the text.

About Reading This Book

In this book, we offer the complete text of Sun Tzu's *The Art of War* on the left-hand pages. The explanation of the text in words and diagrams is on the facing right-hand page. The two pages are meant to be read side-by-side, one with the other, one paragraph at a time. You will be amazed at all the detail hidden in the text you will find using this approach. Sun Tzu's system is incredibly rich in detailed interconnections that are often best described in pictures, which is why diagrams are interjected throughout the book.

Sun Tzu's work has thirteen chapters. Each chapter focuses on a different aspect of the competitive process. The first chapter lays out the basic system. Each succeeding chapter advances a competitive campaign, one step at a time. At their end, many chapters review or preview basic concepts. The final chapter, on information, summarizes the entire system in the context of information flow.

Understanding the text is largely a matter of understanding the context in which Sun Tzu is speaking at any given point. We provide you this context by describing Sun Tzu's concepts in terms of readily understood business concepts. Though Sun Tzu often seems to be discussing physical features of the environment, he is often using those features as an analogy for understanding the abstractions of the competitive process. For example, in his system, water is analogous to change. Even when physical features are being described, useful business analogies are easily found.

As we said earlier, the purpose of this book is to give you a running start in mastering Sun Tzu. However, it certainly doesn't exhaust the ways in which Sun Tzu's ideas can be taught and applied. Clearbridge publishes five other books on *The Art of War*. Our first, *The Art of War: In Sun Tzu's Own Words*, puts the text side-by-side with the original Chinese text translated one character at a time. Reading it gives you an appreciation for the complexities and depth of the original Chinese and why so much that seems "hidden" in English is really there in Chinese.

Three of our other versions adapt the lessons of *The Art of War* to specific business disciplines. One is designed for sales people. Another is for marketing people. The third is for managers working internally within their units to make their people and resources more efficient. We also offer a detailed study guide, called *The Warrior Class*, that explains Sun Tzu, one stanza at a time. Descriptions of these works are provided in the back of this book.

We have also developed a wealth of FREE material explaining Sun Tzu's concepts in detail on our website. We call this on-line classroom, THE WARRIOR CLASS. Access it at www.clearbridge.com. Go to our book owners' area and follow the instructions for finding the needed passwords in this book.

The Competitive Universe

Gary Gagliardi, 2001

The Art of War: PLANNING

This is war.
It is the most important skill in the nation.
It is the basis of life and death.
It is the philosophy of survival or destruction.
You must know it well.

Your skill comes from five factors.
Study these factors when you plan war.
You must insist on knowing the nature of:
1. Military philosophy,
2. The weather,
3. The ground,
4. The commander,
5. And military methods.

It starts with your military philosophy.
Command your people in a way that gives them a higher
shared purpose.
You can lead them to death.
You can lead them to life.
They must never fear danger or dishonesty.

The Amazing Secrets of Competitive Analysis

Though Sun Tzu named his first chapter in Chinese, "Plan Chapter," more accurately it describes the makeup of competitive systems and the most basic rules for successfully using them. What he calls "planning" is closer to what we would describe as competitive analysis.

In many ways, Sun Tzu's work anticipated Darwin in seeing that all competition takes place in an extensive environment. Competition is about systems and how they work. In this paragraph, he sets out the parts of that system as defined by his Five-Element model. We show a picture of this model in the foreword (see page x). It defines the competitive unit within the competitive environment. In Sun Tzu's system, the environment and the competitor are inexorably linked.

For all of us who are competitors, the most important component in this model is the "philosophy" or purpose of our organization. In business, we might call this our corporate mission. Our philosophy must be people-centered, serving the real needs of real people. It must attract employees, customers and other business allies. It must hold the organization together as the source of focus and unity.

Next, you have the weather.
It can be sunny or overcast.
It can be hot or cold.
It includes the timing of the seasons.

Next is the terrain.
It can be distant or near.
It can be difficult or easy.
It can be open or narrow.
It also determines your life or death.

Next is the commander.
He must be smart, trustworthy, caring, brave and strict.

Finally, you have your military methods.
They include the shape of your organization.
This comes from your management philosophy.
You must master their use.

All five of these factors are critical.
As a commander, you must pay attention to them.
Understanding them brings victory.
Ignoring them means defeat.

Though translated here as "weather," the original Chinese character is actually "Heaven." This part of the environment is beyond our control and changes constantly with time. Like the seasons, we can see patterns in it, but we cannot change it.

The terrain or ground is both where we fight and what we fight over. In business, the obvious counterpart is the marketplace. This ground is literally the source of life and all income. Its various characteristics and how to evaluate and use them are the focus of several chapters of *The Art of War*.

The leader creates and defines the competitive unit. A leader's five qualities define the relationships with the other elements.

Our systems, organizations, processes, and procedures are all part of our methods. Methods must be effective, but they must also support the purpose that we serve. They must generate the value defined by our competitive philosophy.

These five key elements are extensively discussed and defined in the course of the book. Each chapter focuses on one or more of these elements. Sun Tzu taught that our success is determined by how well we master these elements.

Qualities of a Leader:
Smart to know the ground.
Brave to face heaven.
Trustworthy & strict in methods.
Caring about philosophy.

Brave Trustworthy

Caring

Smart Strict

You must learn through planning.
You must question the situation.

You must ask:
Which government has the right philosophy?
Which commander has the skill?
Which season and place has the advantage?
Which method of command works?
Which group of forces has the strength?
Which officers and men have the training?
Which rewards and punishments make sense?
This tells when you will win and when you will lose.
Some commanders perform this analysis.
If you use these commanders, you will win.
Keep them.
Some commanders ignore this analysis.
If you use these commanders, you will lose.
Get rid of them.

Plan an advantage by listening.
This makes you powerful.
Get assistance from the outside.
Know the situation.
Then planning can create advantages and controls power.

Sun Tzu believed that we must constantly question our assumptions and conditions in the competitive environment.

Sun Tzu taught that all value is relative. We can never say how "good" anything is in an absolute or abstract sense. We can only compare specific values to real alternatives. We must constantly compare our position and specific abilities to the position and abilities of our real competitors. We don't lose in competition because we do something "wrong." We lose because we don't understand in some fundamental way how we match up with our competition. We must constantly compare our philosophy, our timing, our position, our decision-making, and our procedures with those of our opponents. We will see in later chapters how this relative analysis allows us to match our strengths against an opponent's weaknesses. This alone lets us prioritize an infinite number of possible actions. To be a successful leader, we must insist on working with people who understand how to evaluate our relative conditions.

The foundation of good competitive analysis is knowledge. We must continually open ourselves to new ideas that come in from outside our organization. We must continually work to keep in touch with our competitive environment if we are to survive and find success.

Warfare is one thing.
It is a philosophy of deception.

When you are ready, you try to appear incapacitated.
When active, you pretend inactivity.
When you are close to the enemy, you appear distant.
When far away, pretend you are near.

If the enemy has strong position, entice him away from it.
If the enemy is confused, be decisive.
If the enemy is solid, prepare against him.
If the enemy is strong, avoid him.
If the enemy is angry, frustrate him.
If the enemy is weaker, make him arrogant.
If the enemy is relaxed, make him work.
If the enemy is united, break him apart.
Attack him when he is unprepared.
Leave when he least expects it.

You will find a place where you can win.
Don't pass it by.

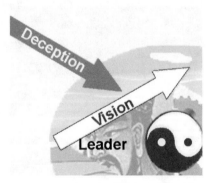

By deception, Sun Tzu does not mean dishonesty. His meaning is closer to controlling people's perceptions.

"Deception," is an attack on vision, that is, seeing opportunities. We control other people's decisions through knowledge. We want to control what they know about us and our intentions. This is how we obtain the decisions that we desire.

We use this "attack" to motivate people to act. Any success we have comes from other people. We must learn how to influence other people's emotions because emotions are the trigger for action. In misleading enemies, we cause them to waste their efforts. Generally, we want to incite people's emotions enough to motivate them into action. Once we can get people moving, they are more easily guided and predicted. Though this section is about working on the emotions of an enemy, the methods work equally well in motivating employees or inspiring customers and partners.

We work to put ourselves into a position where people will do what we desire. When we win this position, we must use it.

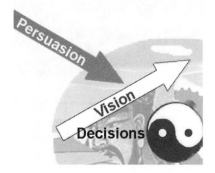

Deception
or Persuasion?
In any terms, an attack aimed at vision and decisions.

9

Before you go to war, you must believe that you can count on victory.
You must calculate many advantages.
Before you go to battle, you may believe that you can foresee defeat.
You can count few advantages.
Many advantages add up to victory.
Few advantages add up to defeat.
How can you know your advantages without analyzing them?
We can see where we are by means of our observations.
We can foresee our victory or defeat by planning.

Success in competition depends on our *vision*, that is, our ability to foresee our relative strength in a specific time and place. Sun Tzu taught that, given an honest evaluation of our strengths and weaknesses, a person with vision can foresee when and where they will be successful. He saw this analysis as a simple mathematical comparison, which is covered in more detail in chapter four. The mistake that most people make is considering only *their own* abilities without considering how these abilities compare with those of the competition. All ability is relative. We have a choice about where and when we compete. We must choose to compete only where and when we can beat any possible competition.

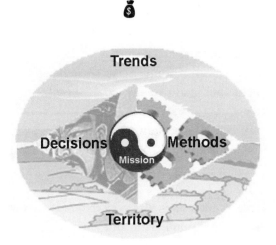

GOING TO WAR

Everything depends on your use of military philosophy.
Moving the army requires thousands of vehicles.
These vehicles must be loaded thousands of times.
The army must carry a huge supply of arms.
You need ten thousand acres of grain.
This results in internal and external shortages.
Any army consumes resources like an invader.
It uses up glue and paint for wood.
It requires armor for its vehicles.
People complain about the waste of a vast amount of metal.
It will set you back when you raise tens of thousands of
troops.

Using a large army makes war very expensive to win.
Long delays create a dull army and sharp defeats.
Attacking enemy cities drains your forces.
Long campaigns that exhaust the nation's resources are
wrong.

This chapter is a critical discussion on the economics of competitive action. Competitive efforts consume resources more intensively than normal productive efforts do. Sales and marketing activities are always more costly than we anticipate. Time and money "invested" on unsuccessful competitive efforts is just wasted. Because competition is so costly, other members of the organization frequently feel that too much time and money is spent on sales and marketing.

Action Means Cost
Costs can make victory
impossible.

The cost of a competitive effort is determined by the size of the effort multiplied by its duration. Striking at an enemy's strong points requires large forces and time. Sun Tzu defines "winning" as making victory pay. If our actions are too costly, costly attacks can never be profitable.

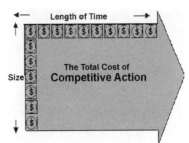

Manage a dull army.
You will suffer sharp defeats.
Drain your forces.
Your money will be used up.
Your rivals multiply as your army collapses and they will
begin against you.
It doesn't matter how smart you are.
You cannot get ahead by taking losses!

You hear of people going to war too quickly.
Still, you won't see a skilled war that lasts a long time.

You can fight a war for a long time or you can make your
nation strong.
You can't do both.

You can never totally understand all the dangers in using
arms.
Therefore, you can never totally understand the advantages
in using arms either.

You want to make good use of war.
Do not raise troops repeatedly.
Do not carry too many supplies.
Choose to be useful to your nation.
Feed off the enemy.
Make your army carry only the provisions it needs.

Sun Tzu taught that economic miscalculations cascade into bigger and bigger problems. He isn't against taking risks and failing, but we can't afford to make large, costly mistakes. In competition, we survive only as long as we have money to continue. When we have money, we have friends. When we don't, the world turns its back on us. Our first priority in competitive action is to preserve our financial resources. We can never spend our way to success.

This means that all competitive actions must be short, limited "tests" to see if they can generate revenue.

We must quickly get to the point where a competitive action generates revenue instead of consuming it. Competition that generates revenue is what strengthens us.

We can never know what a competitive campaign will bring us. It can bring us more success than we can dream of or it can be a total failure. Success demands competitive action, but reason demands financial caution.

Sun Tzu teaches us to be very financially conservative. We must limit our spending. We must do our tasks correctly the first time. We cannot afford to redo them. We can never afford to be extravagant. The less we spend on a competitive effort, the more quickly it can become profitable and start generating revenue instead of consuming resources.

The nation impoverishes itself shipping to troops that are far away.
Distant transportation is costly for hundreds of families.
Buying goods with the army nearby is also expensive.
These high prices also impoverish hundreds of families.
People quickly exhaust their resources supporting a military force.
Military forces consume a nation's wealth entirely.
War leaves households in the former heart of the nation with nothing.

War destroys hundreds of families.
Out of every ten families, war leaves only seven.
War empties the government's storehouses.
Broken armies will get rid of their horses.
They will throw down their armor, helmets, and arrows.
They will lose their swords and shields.
They will leave their wagons without oxen.
War will consume sixty percent of everything you have.

Because of this, the commander's duty is to feed off the enemy.

Use a cup of the enemy's food.
It is worth twenty of your own.
Win a bushel of the enemy's feed.
It is worth twenty of your own.

You can kill the enemy and frustrate him as well.
Take the enemy's strength from him by stealing away his supplies.

Here Sun Tzu adds another dimension to size and time. The third dimension is distance. The more physical distance or space that we try to compete in, the more costly our actions. Distant competitive campaigns must be avoided like large and lengthy campaigns, if we want to be successful.

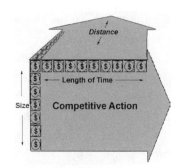

The Three Dimensional Cost Model.

The reality is that competition isn't easy. Most competitors are unsuccessful most of the time. Eighty percent of new businesses fail within the first two years. The loss usually is complete. People lose their entire investment. All care, effort, and value that people try to build up in creating success are lost. In competition, simply putting in the time does not guarantee a return on our investment. We must be successful to realize return on our investment.

ð—🔑

The cost and difficulty of competition means that we must focus on generating revenue from our efforts.

A dollar is not always a dollar. A dollar that we generate from our competitive efforts is worth twenty times more than a dollar that we invest in the business. Only competitive efforts that support themselves are valuable.

Winning in competition is not a matter of beating our competition in a confrontation. It is a matter of taking money out of the territory so that it is not available to our competitors.

17

Fight for the enemy's supply wagons.
Capture their supplies by using overwhelming force.
Reward the first who capture them.
Then change their banners and flags.
Mix them in with your own to increase your supply line.
Keep your soldiers strong by providing for them.
This is what it means to beat the enemy while you grow
more powerful.

Make victory in war pay for itself.
Avoid expensive, long campaigns.
The military commander's knowledge is the key.
It determines if the civilian officials can govern.
It determines if the nation's households are peaceful or a
danger to the state.

No matter what our arena for competition, Sun Tzu teaches that the only meaningful success is financial success. We must *always* focus our efforts on generating revenue. Revenue means that people find what we are doing valuable. Financial success breeds more success. We must reinvest our profits in growing the business. The more money we have, the more we can do. The more financial support we get, the weaker our competition becomes.

Sun Tzu defines success simply as "making victory pay." Making a profit comes in the final step, positioning, but it is determined by the first step, our knowledge. This *knowing* determines our ability to see opportunities with our *vision*. We must be able to find opportunities that have a minimum cost. Inexpensive *actions* lead to profitable *positions*.

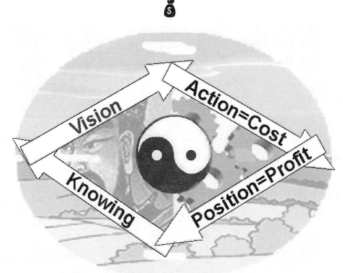

The Profit of Position must Pay the Cost of Action
The purpose of movement is to find profitable positions.

Planning an Attack

Everyone relies on the arts of war.
A united nation is strong.
A divided nation is weak.
A united army is strong.
A divided army is weak.
A united force is strong.
A divided force is weak.
United men are strong.
Divided men are weak.
A united unit is strong.
A divided unit is weak.

Unity works because it enables you to win every battle you fight.
Still, this is the foolish goal of a weak leader.
Avoid battle and make the enemy's men surrender.
This is the right goal for a superior leader.

THE AMAZING SECRETS OF UNITY AND FOCUS

This chapter focuses on the issues we must address before we start a competitive campaign. The first requirement of a campaign is unity and focus. In *Sun Tzu*, these come from our competitive philosophy or mission that brings our people together. Sun Tzu teaches that unity and focus are the source of all strength in competition. An organization is strong when it has a core of shared values.

Philosophy Unites!

The next issue in a competitive campaign is the goal. The goal should never be to confront the competition. The goal should be to win a position that is so powerful that no one challenges us once we have it. Fights are costly. We are looking to develop a valuable position without a confrontation.

Philosophy Focuses!

The best policy is to attack while the enemy is still planning.
The next best is to disrupt alliances.
The next best is to attack the opposing army.
The worst is to attack the enemy's cities.

This is what happens when you attack a city.
You can attempt it, but you can't finish it.
First you must make siege engines.
You need the right equipment and machinery.
You use three months and still cannot win.
Then, you try to encircle the area.
You use three more months without making progress.
The commander still doesn't win and this angers him.
He then tries to swarm the city.
This kills a third of his officers and men.
He still isn't able to draw the enemy out of the city.
This attack is a disaster.

Make good use of war.
Make the enemy's troops surrender.
You can do this fighting only minor battles.
You can draw their men out of their cities.
You can do it with small attacks.
You can destroy the men of a nation.
You must keep your campaign short.

Attacking while planning is another way of using "deception," an attack on *vision*. Disrupting alliances is a *new* attack, one on unity.

The Best Two Attacks

Sun Tzu prioritizes the strength of attacks on the basis of their cost and the relative impact on unity. In chapter one, he said that deception was the heart of war. This is because it catches the competition unaware, moving before they have imagined our action, before they have come together. This is the least expensive type of attack. The next best attack is one that aims directly at an opposing philosophy. This undermines an opponent's unity and focus. This is also an inexpensive attack. The worst attack is an attack on a competitor's developed position, a "siege." This is costly in time and resources, and it attacks where the competition is the most united. This type of attack must always be avoided.

When we are contemplating a competitive action, we must plan to make it quick, small, and local. This keeps our actions united and focused. We don't aim at opponents. We aim at winning territory. We can discuss attacks as targeted at an opponent's

Competitive attacks:
Aimed at new territory, but small quick and close.

various skills; our actions are always really aimed at winning productive territory.

You must use total war, fighting with everything you have.
Never stop fighting when at war.
You can gain complete advantage.
To do this, you must plan your strategy of attack.

The rules for making war are:
If you outnumber the enemy ten to one, surround them.
If you outnumber them five to one, attack them.
If you outnumber them two to one, divide them.
If you are equal, then find an advantageous battle.
If you are fewer, defend against them.
If you are much weaker, evade them.

Small forces are not powerful.
However, large forces cannot catch them.

You must master command.
The nation must support you.

Supporting the military makes the nation powerful.
Not supporting the military makes the nation weak.

Politicians create problems for the military in three different
ways.
Ignorant of the army's inability to advance, they order an
advance.
Ignorant of the army's inability to withdraw, they order a
withdrawal.
We call this tying up the army.
Politicians don't understand the army's business.
Still, they think they can run an army.
This confuses the army's officers.

In competing in small, quick, and local campaigns, we must focus all of our efforts. A winning campaign is never a halfhearted one. We must concentrate all our resources according to the rules that Sun Tzu lists.

Sun Tzu teaches that size is never the source of strength. Strength comes from unity. However, our relative concentration *at a specific time and place* determines our immediate power. Ideally, we focus all our resources on a small competitive arena, completely outnumbering any opposition. When this is not possible, we divide the competition, pick our battles, defend our strong points, and evade the opposition.

The force must be used correctly. Large forces must overpower small ones. Small forces must evade larger ones.

ᛒ─ᚼ

Think of "the nation" as the large, productive part of an organization that is not directly involved in external competition.

Organizations must support external competition in every way to become successful. Those that don't will eventually fail.

Sun Tzu recognizes that conflict between the competitive and noncompetitive (productive) parts of an organization is an inherent problem. He makes it clear that the decisions in competition must be based solely upon competitive reality. We cannot ever make competitive decisions based upon internal needs or interests. The larger competitive environment alone must determine our competitive decisions.

Internal Conflict is Natural.

Politicians don't know the army's chain of command.
They give the army too much freedom.
This will create distrust among the army's officers.

The entire army becomes confused and distrusting.
This invites the invasion from many different rivals.
We say correctly that disorder in an army kills victory.

You must know five things to win:
Victory comes from knowing when to attack and when to
avoid battle.
Victory comes from correctly using large and small forces.
Victory comes from everyone sharing the same goals.
Victory comes from finding opportunities in problems.
Victory comes from having a capable commander and the
government leaving him alone.
You must know these five things.
You then know the theory of victory.

We say:
"Know yourself and know your enemy.
You will be safe in every battle.
You may know yourself but not know the enemy.
You will then lose one battle for every one you win.
You may not know yourself or the enemy.
You will then lose every battle."

When the competitive focus breaks down, so does the organization.

Without unity, the organization as a whole cannot be successful.

Politics Destroys Organizational Unity.

Knowledge is the foundational skill in Sun Tzu's system. Here, he offers five types of knowledge that match up with the Five Elements. Sun Tzu often sums up his chapter's theme in the larger context of his complete system at the chapter's end.

This summarizes the chapter and provides a bit of review.

Sun Tzu is reminding us that all competitive analysis is

Five Types of Knowing:
When of heaven.
Force of methods.
Sharing of philosphy.
Opportunity of ground.
Decisions of leader.

comparative. We must continually compare ourselves to the competition in each of the Five Key Elements in this case, within the large context of local focus and our unity of purpose. We will *never* beat the competition in any area where they are more focused than we are.

POSITIONING

Learn from the history of successful battles.
Your first actions should deny victory to the enemy.
You pay attention to your enemy to find the way to win.
You alone can deny victory to the enemy.
Only your enemy can allow you to win.

You must fight well.
You can prevent the enemy's victory.
You cannot win unless the enemy enables your victory.

We say:
You see the opportunity for victory; you don't create it.

You are sometimes unable to win.
You must then defend.
You will eventually be able to win.
You must then attack.
Defend when you have insufficient strength to win.
Attack when you have more strength than you need to win.

The Amazing Secrets of Awaiting Opportunities

Thus far, the text has focused on attack, but in Sun Tzu's system, attack is not the primary form of competitive action. Sun Tzu believes that most competitions are won on defense rather than offense. That is the topic of this chapter. When he cites history here, he means that statistics favor defense.

Attack is about moving to new positions. Defense in Sun Tzu's system means staying where we are, holding our position. Holding what we have denies our opponents' success.

This is a key concept: we can not create opportunity. Our skill at vision sees opportunity. Don't waste effort trying to build it.

According to Sun Tzu's methods, we don't really decide whether to attack or defend. We should normally be thinking about defending what we have. We must not attack unless we have more resources than we need to defend. Then, if we see a *clear* opportunity, one where we can't lose, then we *must* attack.

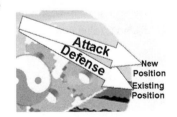

29

You must defend yourself well.
Save your forces and dig in.
You must attack well.
Move your forces when you have a clear advantage.

You must protect your forces until you can completely
triumph.

Some may see how to win.
However, they cannot position their forces where they must.
This demonstrates limited ability.

Some can struggle to a victory and the whole world may
praise their winning.
This also demonstrates a limited ability.

Win as easily as picking up a fallen hair.
Don't use all of your forces.
See the time to move.
Don't try to find something clever.
Hear the clap of thunder.
Don't try to hear something subtle.

Learn from the history of successful battles.
Victory goes to those who make winning easy.
A good battle is one that you will obviously win.
It doesn't take intelligence to win a reputation.
It doesn't take courage to achieve success.

Survival depends on choosing the right ground. We move to ground that is easy to defend. We hold it until we find a better position.

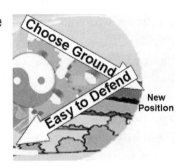

New Position

A position is a survival stepping stone to longer-term success.

Attacking means knowing how to move to a new position. If we cannot move, we cannot succeed

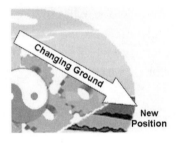

New Position

The failure here is in picking a difficult battle. We must choose positions that are *easy* to win.

Sun Tzu taught that the world is full of opportunities. We must choose only the easiest contests, those most certain of success. The "time to move" is when the trends are in our favor. The "clap of thunder" is clear, unmistakable knowledge. Sun Tzu uses certain analogies consistently. Sight equals vision. Sound equals knowledge. Time equals heaven.

When Sun Tzu refers to "history," he means the past, but he also means the statistical probability of success. When it is a question of survival, we must always bet on certainties. If we don't, we will eventually have a run of "bad luck" that will cost us everything. Choose safe rather than brave or clever.

You must win your battles without effort.
Avoid difficult struggles.
Fight when your position must win.
You always win by preventing your defeat.

You must engage only in winning battles.
Position yourself where you cannot lose.
Never waste an opportunity to defeat your enemy.

You win a war by first assuring yourself of victory.
Only afterward do you look for a fight.
Outmaneuver the enemy before the battle and then fight to win.

You must make good use of war.
Study military philosophy and the art of defense.
You can control your victory or defeat.

This is the art of war.
1. Discuss the distances.
2. Discuss your numbers.
3. Discuss your calculations.
4. Discuss your decisions.
5. Discuss victory.
The ground determines the distance.
The distance determines your numbers.
Your numbers determine your calculations.
Your calculations determine your decisions.
Your decisions determine your victory.

Survival requires thinking both in the short and long term. When we take a position, we are betting on the success of that position over time. Our position must keep us safe until the opposition makes a mistake.

When the opposition does make a mistake and leaves us an opening for a new position, we must move to that new position. If the new position will win us new territory, we must take it.

It is all about winning in the long term—winning the war, not the battle. You can win a difficult battle. No one wins difficult wars—everyone loses. We must keep the costs low and the potential returns high if we expect to win in the long run.

We don't control our environment, but we do control our choice of ground. When we choose our ground, we decide our success or failure.

The equation below is the centerpiece of Sun Tzu's system. Using it, we can calculate exactly when and where we can be successful. It starts with distance, that is, how quickly and easily we can move into a certain position. Small forces have the advantage here. Next comes the amount of resources we can focus on the chosen position. Large organization may have an advantage here. When we compare which organization can focus the most resources at a particular position at a specific time, we can know which of two competitors will win that position. We don't succeed simply by accumulating more force or pushing people, we win by picking the right position.

Creating a winning war is like balancing a coin of gold against a coin of silver.
Creating a losing war is like balancing a coin of silver against a coin of gold.

Winning a battle is always a matter of people.
You pour them into battle like a flood of water pouring into a deep gorge.
This is a matter of positioning.

Sun Tzu's system is dynamic. It assumes that competing forces are constantly moving resources into different positions. The secret to winning is focusing these resources at profitable locations where the competition cannot compete.

Sun Tzu often summarizes at the end of a chapter, but here he is giving us a preview of the topic of the next chapter, MOMENTUM. Positioning and momentum together are what give people success in competition.

The Picture is Static,
But Everything Changes:
Our current view of our competitive environment is just
a snapshot of a constantly changing system.

Momentum

You control a large army as you control a few men.
You just divide their ranks correctly.
You fight a large army the same as you fight a small one.
You only need the right position and communication.
You may meet a large enemy army.
You must be able to encounter the enemy without being defeated.
You must correctly use both surprise and direct action.
Your army's position must increase your strength.
Troops flanking an enemy can smash them like eggs.
You must correctly use both strength and weakness.

It is the same in all battles.
You use a direct approach to engage the enemy.
You use surprise to win.

You must use surprise for a successful invasion.
Surprise is as infinite as the weather and land.
Surprise is as inexhaustible as the flow of a river.

The Amazing Secrets of Innovation

The rules of competition don't change with the size of our organization. What tends to break down with size is position and communication. While Sun Tzu teaches that we should avoid battles, he recognizes that direct confrontations occur. His definition of a "battle" is meeting a competitor's actions with actions of our own. To succeed, battles must be combined with another form of attack, *surprise*.

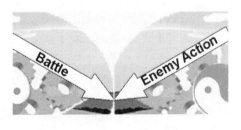

Sun Tzu defines surprise as an attack on enemy knowledge. We best think of it as *innovation*, outmoding existing knowledge and ideas by creative invention.

Sun Tzu taught that there is always an infinite amount of territory, trends, and human creativity for innovation.

37

You can be stopped and yet recover the initiative.
You must use your days and months correctly.

If you are defeated, you can recover.
You must use the four seasons correctly.

There are only a few notes in the scale.
Yet, you can always rearrange them.
You can never hear every song of victory.

There are only a few basic colors.
Yet, you can always mix them.
You can never see all the shades of victory.

There are only a few flavors.
Yet, you can always blend them.
You can never taste all the flavors of victory.

You fight with momentum.
There are only a few types of surprises and direct actions.
Yet, you can always vary the ones you use.
There is no limit in the ways you can win.

Surprise and direct action give birth to each other.
They proceed from each other in an endless cycle.
You can not exhaust all their possible combinations!

The secret to recovering lost momentum is constant innovation. Momentum demands this type of *surprise*.

Successful innovation requires continuous improvement. We cannot pull surprises out of a hat without preparation.

Though his method of rearranging basic ideas to come up with innovations sound poetic, these three stanza tell us that first comes observation (knowing) symbolized by sound.

Then comes inspiration (vision), which is symbolized by sight.

Finally comes testing and evaluation (action, positioning) or tasting.

Though innovation is infinite, a limited

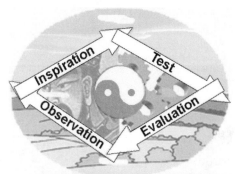

The Skill Cycle as Scientific Method

number of steps in our methods means we can easily change one or another of them to see what works.

Sun Tzu taught that we never battle without surprise and never surprise unless we are in a battle. These two "attacks" work together in an endless cycle.

Attacking Action and Knowledge at Once.

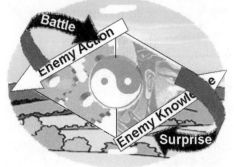

39

Surging water flows together rapidly.
Its pressure washes away boulders.
This is momentum.

A hawk suddenly strikes a bird.
Its contact alone kills the prey.
This is timing.

You must fight only winning battles.
Your momentum must be overwhelming.
Your timing must be exact.

Your momentum is like the tension of a bent crossbow.
Your timing is like the pulling of a trigger.

War is complicated and confused.
Battle is chaotic.
Nevertheless, you must not allow chaos.

War is sloppy and messy.
Positions turn around.
Nevertheless, you must never be defeated.

Chaos gives birth to control.
Fear gives birth to courage.
Weakness gives birth to strength.

You must control chaos.
This depends on your planning.
Your men must brave their fears.
This depends on their momentum.

Momentum means change. The force of battle is not enough.

We must know when to bring a shocking surprise into the action.

The force of battle and the shock of surprise create momentum.

Two Attacks: One Process
Battle and surprise are used one after the other.

Using momentum requires timing.

All competition is chaotic because it arises out of conflict.

Competitive action is unpredictable because our plans collide with the opposing plans of others. This is a naturally sloppy process.

The chaotic nature of competition means we must look for ways to gain control. If we plan predictable surprises, we can seize the initiative and turn around any showdown with competitors.

Sun Tzu's method depends on our preparing innovations before a battle. In unleashing these surprises in a planned way, we get momentum on our side during the critical turning point of a battle. We know what is coming. The opposition doesn't.

You have strengths and weaknesses.
These come from your position.

You must force the enemy to move to your advantage.
Use your position.
The enemy must follow you.
Surrender a position.
The enemy must take it.
You can offer an advantage to move him.
You can use your men to move him.
You use your strength to hold him.

You want a successful battle.
To do this, you must seek momentum.
Do not just demand a good fight from your people.
You must pick good people and then give them momentum.

You must create momentum.
You create it with your men during battle.
This is comparable to rolling trees and stones.
Trees and stones roll because of their shape and weight.
Offer men safety and they will stay calm.
Endanger them and they will act.
Give them a place and they will hold.
Round them up and they will march.

You make your men powerful in battle with momentum.
This is just like rolling round stones down over a high, steep cliff.
Use your momentum.

Our position always gives us the potential for success if we have chosen the position correctly.

We want our opponents reacting to our decisions. The entire point of using surprise during a battle is to seize the initiative and take control of the situation. Otherwise, we are put in the position of having to react to our opponent's actions. We use changes in our position to continually keep our opponents off balance. Since we plan our surprises ahead of time, we can lure our opponents into traps. If we continually do this while confronting opponents, we can force them to fight our strengths.

Notice that none of Sun Tzu's methods involve simply exhorting people to work harder or do better.

Shared Self-Interest:
Our philosphy defines how we all profit from working together.

People

Centered

Instead, he urges us to adopt a philosophy that is people-centered, accepting people as they really are. This means that we must address everyone's basic self-interest. We use momentum and position, the topics of this chapter and the last, to put people in the right place and then put them in motion in the right direction. We ask them only to do what comes naturally in their situation.

This echoes the closing of the previous chapter. There the lesson was that people need good positioning. The idea here is that in order to get the most out of people, we must use both that winning position and give them momentum.

WEAKNESS AND STRENGTH

Always arrive first to the empty battlefield to await the enemy at your leisure.
If you are late and hurry to the battlefield, fighting is more difficult.

You want a successful battle.
Move your men, but not into opposing forces.

You can make the enemy come to you.
Offer him an advantage.
You can make the enemy avoid coming to you.
Threaten him with danger.

When the enemy is fresh, you can tire him.
When he is well fed, you can starve him.
When he is relaxed, you can move him.

The Amazing Secrets of Competitive Relativity

In the original Chinese text, the contrasting ideas of weakness-emptiness and strength-fullness are united. Strength equals abundance. Weakness equals need. Ground that is empty or weak creates the strength of a competitor positioned there.

The reverse is also true: the fullness of an area creates potential weakness in a competitor moving into that area.

Sun Tzu earlier introduced the idea of taking the initiative to control our opponents. Here, he extends that concept to using apparent emptiness (opportunity) to attract competition and apparent abundance (threat) to repel them.

Fullness is being satisfied—here, in the sense of physically satisfied. Satisfaction creates weakness and laziness. All *fullness is temporary.*

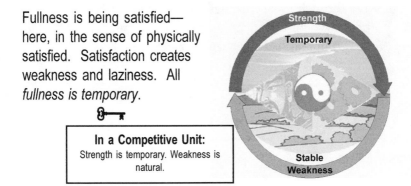

In a Competitive Unit:
Strength is temporary. Weakness is natural.

45

Leave any place without haste.
Hurry to where you are unexpected.
You can easily march hundreds of miles without tiring.
To do so, travel through areas that are deserted.
You must take whatever you attack.
Attack when there is no defense.
You must have walls to defend.
Defend where it is impossible to attack.

Be skilled in attacking.
Give the enemy no idea of where to defend.

Be skillful in your defense.
Give the enemy no idea of where to attack.

Be subtle! Be subtle!
Arrive without any clear formation.
Quietly! Quietly!
Arrive without a sound.
You must use all your skill to control the enemy's decisions.

Advance where they can't defend.
Charge through their openings.
Withdraw where the enemy cannot chase you.
Move quickly so that they cannot catch you.

Since the territory supplies our strength, we must leave established areas slowly and establish new ones quickly. Emptiness saves costs since we move quickly through empty areas. In business, we can think of empty areas as needy customers.

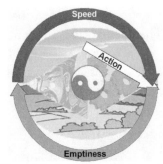

Move into Emptiness for Speed.

Our ability to take territory from the competition requires them to leave those areas empty, needy, and, therefore, undefended.

Our ability to hold a territory depends upon our ability to fill or satisfy that area so there are no openings for the competition.

8—r

Contradicting the fashion of noisy self-promotion, Sun Tzu teaches us to keep quiet, invisible to the enemy. Sound is Sun Tzu's metaphor for knowledge. Strength comes from knowledge, so we must keep our opponents ignorant. We control others by controlling knowledge.

We have two choices about how we can move toward emptiness. We can attack, that is, move into enemy territory, but only if they leave us an opening. We can also elude the enemy, moving away from them more quickly than they can follow.

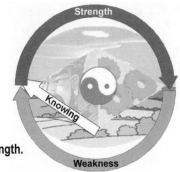

Knowing Creates Strength.

47

I always pick my own battles.
The enemy can hide behind high walls and deep trenches.
I do not try to win by fighting him directly.
Instead, I attack a place that he must rescue.
I avoid the battles that I don't want.
I can divide the ground and yet defend it.
I don't give the enemy anything to win.
Divert him from coming to where you defend.

I make their men take a position while I take none.
I then focus my forces where the enemy divides his forces.
Where I focus, I unite my forces.
When the enemy divides, he creates many small groups.
I want my large group to attack one of his small ones.
Then I have many men where the enemy has but a few.
My large force can overwhelm his small one.
I then go on to the next small enemy group.
I will take them one at a time.

We must keep the place that we've chosen as a
battleground a secret.
The enemy must not know.
Force the enemy to prepare his defense in many places.
I want the enemy to defend many places.
Then I can choose where to fight.
His forces will be weak there.

48

We must see our position as dynamic, something we must shift at will. The principle of emptiness and fullness determines where we put our resources. We never move against the opponent's strong points. Instead, we look for places they need and that they have left needy and undefended. "Dividing a territory" means focusing on a small segment. If we don't want a confrontation, we empty an area, leaving the opposition nothing to win there.

Focus Creates Knowing and Strength.

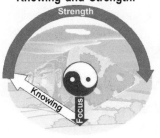

Fullness and its resulting strength are related directly to unity and, especially, to focus. Most organizations try to protect too much territory, making their forces weak and positions empty. The solution to this is to bring our forces together and focus them in a very specific, small area. This allows us to pick off the diluted competition.

Again, emptiness and fullness depend on knowledge. In the skill cycle, the initial step is knowledge. Action without knowledge is wasted. Without a strong, central focus, organizations spread out, defending many different places. Trying to defend too much ground creates weakness.

Spreading out Creates Weakness.

49

If he reinforces his front lines, he depletes his rear.
If he reinforces his rear, he depletes his front.
If he reinforces his right, he depletes his left.
If he reinforces his left, he depletes his right.
Without knowing the place of attack, he cannot prepare.
Without a place, he will be weak everywhere.

The enemy has weak points.
Prepare your men against them.
He has strong points.
Make his men prepare themselves against you.

You must know the battle ground.
You must know the time of battle.
You can then travel a thousand miles and still win the battle.

The enemy should not know the battleground.
He shouldn't know the time of battle.
His left will be unable to support his right.
His right will be unable to support his left.
His front lines will be unable to support his rear.
His rear will be unable to support his front.
His support is distant even if it is only ten miles away.
What unknown place can be close?

We control the balance of forces.
The enemy may have many men but they are superfluous.
How can they help him to victory?

Shifting resources around within an overly large area is not the same as focus. Focus is concentration. Shifting creates pockets of temporary strength and pockets of weakness.

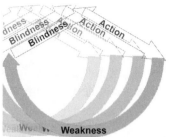

Action without Vision.

The choices we make are ultimately simple. We focus our resources on areas of need, emptiness. We don't let the competition know so that they cannot counteract our focus in time to be effective against us.

⚷

The point here is that emptiness is not just a matter of place. Since situations are dynamic and constantly changing, it is a matter of both time and place. Needs change continuously.

We must keep our true focus secret. Fullness, strength, and our ability to satisfy a market come from our focus on the emptiness in a specific time and place. When we choose our focus, we must realize that our opportunity is only temporary. However, the fact that we know the focus—and our opponents do not—gives us all the advantage that we need. After we win our position, competitive reactions are too late to have any effect. We need to keep our opponents one step behind us.

We must take the initiative in competition. By determining the basis or ground for competition, we can concentrate our efforts successfully and force the enemy to react to us.

We say:
You must let victory happen.

The enemy may have many men.
You can still control him without a fight.

When you form your strategy, know the strengths and weaknesses of your plan.
When you execute, know how to manage both action and inaction.
When you take a position, know the deadly and the winning grounds.
When you battle, know when you have too many or too few men.

Use your position as your war's centerpiece.
Arrive at the battle without a formation.
Don't take a position.
Then even the best spies can't report it.
Even the wisest general cannot plan to counter you.
Take a position where you can triumph using superior numbers.
Keep the enemy's forces ignorant.
Their troops will learn of my location when my position will win.
They must not know how our location gives us a winning position.
Make the battle one from which they cannot recover.
You must always adjust your position to their position.

We must be opportunistic. We must take what opponents give us, and accept what we are given, instead of looking for fights.

We have control over the contest when we pick the place where we have the local advantage.

Here, Sun Tzu lists the skills of vision (planning), action, and positioning and explains their empty and full states. For each of these skills, we must *know* how to manage both its strengths and its weaknesses. This is why knowling is the foundation of all other skills.

Knowing Has No Empty State.

Positioning is the end result of all our other competitive skills. In positioning, our success does not come *only* from our own abilities. It comes from the qualities of the ground that we have chosen *and* our ability to use it. In other words, the power that we have comes from how well we use our environment by picking our niche. To serve us, the position that we choose must be empty. This means that any potential competition cannot guess our plans, or they will move to fill the space that we see. This means that the most important competitive skill that we must disable is enemy vision. When we confront the opposition, we must be more powerful in our chosen time and place.

"Ground" Skills Create Strength.

Manage your military position like water.
Water takes every shape.
It avoids the high and moves to the low.
Your war can take any shape.
It must avoid the strong and strike the weak.
Water follows the shape of the land that directs its flow.
Your forces follow the enemy who determines how you win.

Make war without a standard approach.
Water has no consistent shape.
If you follow the enemy's shifts and changes, you can always win.
We call this shadowing.

Fight five different campaigns without a firm rule for victory.
Use all four seasons without a consistent position.
Your timing must be sudden.
A few weeks determine your failure or success.

Water is Sun Tzu's analogy for change. Water is perfect for this chapter's focus on the dynamics of competitive positioning. Here, the adaptability of water stands for opportunism in competition. As positions of weakness and strength change, we must continuously shift toward the weakness, the need. We do not determine where the weakness is. The ground, the market, the needs of others determine where there is need.

The main focus of this chapter has been positioning and the ground, but here Sun Tzu reminds us that finding positions is a function of our creativity and our skill at vision. This stanza also introduces a critical idea of keeping up with opponents until we can see an opening by which to surpass them.

Time and the seasons fall within the realm of heaven (trends over time). We do not control these trends, but we can foresee them if we have vision. We must wait through the empty times for the fullness of time that brings opportunity. When opportunity appears, we must grab it before change takes it away.

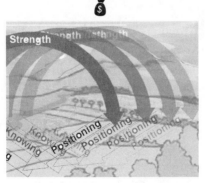

A Position of Strength Leads to More Strength.

Armed Conflict

Everyone uses the arts of war.
You accept orders from the government.
Then you assemble your army.
You organize your men and build camps.
You must avoid disasters from armed conflict.

Seeking armed conflict can be disastrous.
Because of this, a detour can be the shortest path.
Because of this, problems can become opportunities.

Use an indirect route as your highway.
Use the search for advantage to guide you.
When you fall behind, you must catch up.
When you get ahead, you must wait.
You must know the detour that most directly accomplishes your plan.

Undertake armed conflict when you have an advantage.
Seeking armed conflict for its own sake is dangerous.

THE AMAZING SECRETS OF DIRECT CONFRONTATION

Sun Tzu makes it clear in this chapter that conflict is not the same as competition. We can be successful in competition while avoiding confrontation and conflict. We prepare for confrontation, but our goal is always to avoid it.

We can seek gain and still avoid conflict. Conflict takes time and energy. It is damaging and *costly*. By avoiding conflict, we can move quickly and conserve our resources.

We must initially concentrate our resources on developing our position and advantage. It is our position that enriches us, not conflict. We can afford to change our plans to avoid unnecessary direct confrontations.

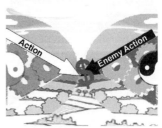

Conflict is Costly:
Competition is more than conflict.

When our position is secure, we can accept that some confrontations are unavoidable, but they are always costly.

You can build up an army to fight for an advantage.
Then you won't catch the enemy.
You can force your army to go fight for an advantage.
Then you abandon your heavy supply wagons.

You keep only your armor and hurry straight after the
enemy.
You avoid stopping day or night.
You use many roads at the same time.
You go hundreds of miles to fight for an advantage.
Then the enemy catches your commanders and your army.
Your strong soldiers get there first.
Your weaker soldiers follow behind.
Using this approach, only one in ten will arrive.
You can try to go fifty miles to fight for an advantage.
Then your commanders and army will stumble.
Using this method, only half of your soldiers will make it.
You can try to go thirty miles to fight for an advantage.
Then only two out of three get there.

If you make your army travel without good supply lines,
they will die.
Without supplies and food, your army will die.
If you don't save the harvest, your army will die.

Here, Sun Tzu examines the folly of trying to *force* direct confrontations to create opportunities. When we have a large enough force to win, we are too slow. To move quickly when we are large, we have to abandon our infrastructure.

By definition, when we try to build a larger force than that of the opposition, we are also building a force that is slower than the opposition. How does such a force catch up for a direct confrontation? The only solution is "hurry," that is, leaving stuff behind and pressing your people to go faster. Sun Tzu teaches that

Small = Fast

Large=Slow

Hurry = Stretch & Break
Conflict is Unnatural
Small is fast. Large is slow. Large falls apart if it hurries.

hurry destroys the unity of a large force, negating its supposed strength.

This stanza is all about infrastructure: the cash, supplies, and structures that we need to *sustain* our organization over time. "Hurry" disregards the need for infrastructure. This is always fatal for an organization. Organizations need their supply lines.

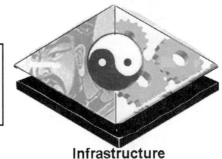

Organizations Depend on Infrastructure.
Much of what makes them work is hidden below the surface.

Infrastructure

Do not let any of your potential enemies know of what you are planning.
Still, you must not hesitate to form alliances.
You must know the lay of the land.
You must know where the obstructions are.
You must know where the marshes are.
If you don't, you cannot move the army.
You must use local guides.
If you don't, you can't take advantage of the terrain.

You make war using a deceptive position.
If you use deception, then you can move.
Using deception, you can upset the enemy and change the situation.
You must move as quickly as the wind.
You must rise like the forest.
You must invade and plunder like fire.
You must stay as motionless as a mountain.
You must be as mysterious as the fog.
You must strike like sounding thunder.

Divide your troops to plunder the villages.
When on open ground, dividing is an advantage.
Don't worry about organization, just move.
Be the first to find a new route that leads directly to a winning plan.
This is the how you are successful at armed conflict.

Instead of looking for confrontations, we should hide from the enemy. We must use our ground, that is, our territory or market. Knowing the ground is another source of speed. Joining allies is an alternative source of size. The ground is the source of

Hide from Opposition.

positions that we can easily and inexpensively build up. The ground, not conflict, is the source of success.

Using a "deceptive position" means simply that we should keep our competitive intent a secret so that we can develop our ground. Our goals must be secret. If we eliminate costly confrontations, we are free to put our resources into profitable efforts. Most of the metaphors used here relate to developing our position, but they start with moving into position. If we are hidden, we can move into new areas without interference. We can then build our position. We can get income from our territory. We can hold it effortlessly. We can instantly act with certain knowledge (the thunderclap).

Unity gives us strength in confrontations, but it is not needed if we avoid confrontations. Instead of focusing, we can spread out, divide our time and resources among several different tasks. This allows us to get the benefit of more ground, more quickly. Developing empty territory demands that we get to the area first. The irony here is that the way we get the benefit from armed conflict is by avoiding it.

We Can Spread Out on Empty Ground.

Military experience says:
"You can speak, but you will not be heard.
You must use gongs and drums.
You cannot really see your forces just by looking.
You must use banners and flags."

You must master gongs, drums, banners and flags.
Place people as a single unit where they can all see and hear.
You must unite them as one.
Then, the brave cannot advance alone.
The fearful cannot withdraw alone.
You must force them to act as a group.

In night battles, you must use numerous fires and drums.
In day battles, you must use many banners and flags.
You must position your people to control what they see and
hear.

You control your army by controlling its emotions.
As a general, you must be able to control emotions.

In the morning, a person's energy is high.
During the day, it fades.
By evening, a person's thoughts turn to home.
You must use your troops wisely.
Avoid the enemy's high spirits.
Strike when they are lazy and want to go home.
This is how you master energy.

Sun Tzu changes the topic from avoiding armed conflict to winning at these direct confrontations when we can't avoid them. The first key to winning a conflict is communication. Sun Tzu believes that communication is difficult and that to be successful we must amplify it.

The purpose of all communication in Sun Tzu's system is group unity. In confrontation especially, it is our unity that gives us strength.

Communication Creates Unity in Battle.

Execution depends on communication, so we must be able to communicate in every situation. Part of choosing a position means considering its utility for communication.

After communication, the second most important key in confrontation is controlling emotions.

The first part of emotions is energy. Controlling emotional energy is largely a function of using the correct timing. In Sun Tzu's system, timing requires understanding the trends of the moment. This means vision.

One aspect of vision is our ability to inspire people, and conversely, to discourage our competitors.

Control During Conflict
Know, inspire, avoid action, and stand your ground.

63

Use discipline to await the chaos of battle.
Keep relaxed to await a crisis.
This is how you master emotion.

Stay close to home to await a distant enemy.
Stay comfortable to await the weary enemy.
Stay well fed to await the hungry enemy.
This is how you master power.

Don't entice the enemy when their ranks are orderly.
You must not attack when their formations are solid
This is how you master adaptation.
You must follow these military rules.
Do not take a position facing the high ground.
Do not oppose those with their backs to wall.
Do not follow those who pretend to flee.
Do not attack the enemy's strongest men.
Do not swallow the enemy's bait.
Do not block an army that is heading home.
Leave an escape outlet for a surrounded army.
Do not press a desperate foe.
This is the art of war.

In conflict, what we don't do is as important as what we do. This point is made more forcefully at the end of the chapter; the point here is that we must not get caught up in emotion.

The last part of controlling emotions is planning confrontations so that we properly harness the powers of emptiness and fullness. Everyone is more comfortable staying close to home. If we have the good ground, we will have the power.

This last stanza starts with a look forward to the next section on adaptability. Adaptability is our ability to change our plans based upon our opportunities. Here, the philosophy of adaptability addresses avoiding confrontations when our opponents are in a strong or controlling position. These rules follow many of the issues that we have covered. We never confront a strong position. We never let enemy actions dictate the flow of events. We never force confrontations that are so costly that our opponents cannot afford to lose them. In other words, when we cannot avoid direct confrontations, we must manage them so that we have a decent chance of winning. It is never just our strength that matters; it is our relationship to our opponent's strengths and weaknesses.

Conflicting Plans
Our plans are not perfectly predictable because our opponents also have plans. Both sets of plans come into conflict.

Adaptability

Everyone uses the arts of war.
As a general, you get your orders from the government.
You gather your troops.
On dangerous ground, you must not camp.
Where the roads intersect, you must join your allies.
When an area is cut off, you must not delay in it.
When you are surrounded, you must scheme.
In a life-of-death situation, you must fight.
There are roads that you must not take.
There are armies that you must not fight.
There are strongholds that you must not attack.
There are positions that you must not defend.
There are government commands that must not be obeyed.

Military leaders must be experts in knowing how to adapt to win.
This will teach you the use of war.

The Amazing Secrets of Opportunism

This chapter is best understood as an introduction to the next three chapters, which give a great deal of information about specific situations and how to respond to them. Sun Tzu's concept of planning means adjusting to our changing situation. We must be

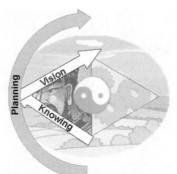

Planning is Knowing with Vision:
Analysis not To-do Lists.

opportunistic. Opportunism requires recognizing common situations and knowing instantly how we must respond to them. Sun Tzu mandates creativity, but in many competitive situations the leader is required to know the correct response.

The foundation of all action and non-action is our knowledge as decision-makers. We must know all these common situations, recognize them, and respond to them appropriately.

Know right response:
See the situation and respond.

Some commanders are not good at making adjustments to
find an advantage.
They can know the shape of the terrain.
Still, they can not find an advantageous position.

Some military commanders do not know how to adjust their
methods.
They can find an advantageous position.
Still, they can not use their men effectively.

You must be creative in your planning.
You must adapt to your opportunities and weaknesses.
You can use a variety of approaches and still have a
consistent result.
You must adjust to a variety of problems and consistently
solve them.

You can deter your potential enemy by using his weaknesses
against him.
You can keep your enemy's army busy by giving it work to
do.
You can rush your enemy by offering him an advantageous
position.

Other than ignorance, decision-makers have two problems with adaptability. The first is that they don't see *where* to move.

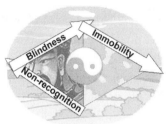

The second problem with adaptability is that, despite seeing what needs to be done, the organization is unable to do it well enough to be effective.

8——⚡

Here, Sun Tzu is telling us that, despite the need for a specific type of response, creativity is still a vital part of our approach. We can vary our methods despite the need for a clear-cut type of action. Our goal must be consistent results, but we must adjust our responses to the situation to achieve that goal.

8——⚡

We must always take the initiative in every situation. Rather than responding to our opponents' moves, we must force them to react to our moves. To do this, we must understand their needs or weaknesses. Our opponents are motivated by the emotions of fear and greed. In the upcoming chapter, we will be given many specific examples of how to understand the competition's motives.

8——⚡

> **Understand the Oppositions' Needs to Predict their Actions.**

69

You must make use of war.
Do not trust that the enemy isn't coming.
Trust on your readiness to meet him.
Do not trust that the enemy won't attack.
We must rely only on our ability to pick a place that the
enemy can't attack.

You can exploit five different faults in a leader.
If he is willing to die, you can kill him.
If he wants to survive, you can capture him.
He may have a quick temper.
You can then provoke him with insults.
If he has a delicate sense of honor, you can disgrace him.
If he loves his people, you can create problems for him.
In every situation, look for these five weaknesses.
They are common faults in commanders.
They always lead to military disaster.

To overturn an army, you must kill its general.
To do this, you must use these five weaknesses.
You must always look for them.

Skill in adaptability means that we are *always* prepared for the worst. Sun Tzu forces us to assume that our competition is every bit as capable as we are. As the situation changes, we must assume that the competition knows how to take advantage of it. The secret to success is survival. We must survive long enough for an opportunity to present itself.

The five flaws of a leader correlate directly with his or her relationship to the other elements in Sun Tzu's Five Element Model. They are direct counterparts to the qualities of a leader listed in chapter one. Fearlessness comes from too much faith in our position in the world. Fearfulness comes from too little faith in future trends. Over-attachment and a bad temper are overreactions to our methods and people. A "delicate sense of honor" is being too sensitive about our philosophy or beliefs. We can take competition seriously without overreacting to our situation. As a leader we must moderate our reactions.

Our leadership flaws are only meaningful when compared to those of the competition. We may be afraid, but we are only fearful if we are more afraid than our competitors.

Faults of a Leader:
Defined by relationship with the other Elements. Compare with the qualities of a leader on page five.

71

Armed March

Everyone moving their army must adjust to the enemy.

Keep out of the mountains and in the valleys.
Position yourself on the heights facing the sun.
To win your battles, never attack uphill.
This is how you position your army in the mountains.

When water blocks you, keep far away from it.
Let the enemy cross the river and wait for him.
Do not meet him in midstream.
Wait for him to get half his forces across and then take
advantage of the situation.

You need to be able to fight.
You can't do that if you are in the water when you meet an
attack.
Position yourself upstream, facing the sun.
Never face against the current.
Always position your army upstream when near the water.

THE AMAZING SECRETS OF COMPETITIVE EXPLORATION

This chapter is about moving into new competitive areas.

Sun Tzu talks about mountains, water, marshes, and level plains, but these are also good metaphors. Mountains are business areas dealing with large corporations or big government. We don't fight mountains and make progress in their lower levels.

Water is Sun Tzu's metaphor for change. Think of rivers and streams as fluid areas where people have to deal with change. Fashion, music, film, and high-tech industries are very fluid. Businesses in these areas must constantly deal with change in order to survive.

High change areas are difficult, but we still can compete in them. If we are in a high-change business or in a business transition, we must use the "currents," that is, trends of change, in our favor. This is very much the same as the way we use gravity and height in the mountains.

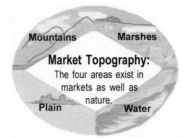

Market Topography:
The four areas exist in markets as well as nature.

73

You may have to move across marshes.
Move through them quickly without stopping.
You may meet the enemy in the middle of a marsh.
You must keep on the water grasses.
Keep your back to a clump of trees.
This is how you position your army in a marsh.

On a level plateau, take a position that you can change.
Keep the higher ground on your right and to the rear.
Keep the danger in front of you and safety behind.
This is how you position yourself on a level plateau.

You can find an advantage in all four of these situations.
Learn from the great emperor who used positioning to
conquer his four rivals.

Armies are stronger on high ground and weaker on low.
They are better camping on sunny, southern hillsides than on
the shady, northern ones.
Provide for your army's health and place it well.
Your army will be free from disease.
Done correctly, this means victory.

You must sometimes defend on a hill or riverbank.
You must keep on the south side in the sun.
Keep the uphill slope at your right rear.

This will give the advantage to your army.
It will always give you a position of strength.

Marshes are unstable or risky areas. Think of a financially troubled or shifting market segment. Industries that depend on chance—such as farming or venture capital—are also marshes. They are not ideal competitive arenas, but we can compete in them if we find islands of stability that we can count on and protect our backs.

Think of flat areas as broad markets with many customers of equal importance. This is good ground for exploration. In these situations, you face problems. Problems are where opportunities lie. You move with the flow of the ground.

In these general conditions, our opponents are on the same footing as we are. If we use better approaches than our competitors, we can be successful in any of them.

Height translates to higher positions in an organization or larger companies within a marketplace. Think of "sunny" as a metaphor for visible. People are healthier and happier when they have the support of top people, large customers, and when they are getting market visibility. This is a psychological issue as well as a financial one.

We should defend any advantage that we have. We can do this by using visibility and height.

Uneveness **Market** Uncertainty
Topography:
Markets can be characterized by their makeup.

Evenness   Change

According to Sun Tzu's methods, we want to be the big, shiny fish in a small pond.

Stop the march when the rain swells the river into rapids.
You may want to ford the river.
Wait until it subsides.

All regions have dead-ends such as waterfalls.
There are deep lakes.
There are high cliffs.
There are dense jungles.
There are thick quagmires.
There are steep crevasses.
Get away from all these quickly.
Do not get close to them.
Keep them at a distance.
Maneuver the enemy close to them.
Position yourself facing these dangers.
Push the enemy back into them.

Danger can hide on your army's flank.
There are reservoirs and lakes.
There are reeds and thickets.
There are forests of trees.
Their dense vegetation provides a hiding place.
You must cautiously search through them.
They can always hide an ambush.

Challenging periods of change can affect any situation and any industry. When they come, we should hold our current position and not try to move to a new one.

Each position that we take must be a stepping stone to a new position. For this to work, we must avoid any dead-end positions. We should avoid fundamental transitions, big changes in size, business gambles, and other risks. Sun Tzu teaches us to avoid risky areas in general. We should leave all the risky "opportunities" for our competition.

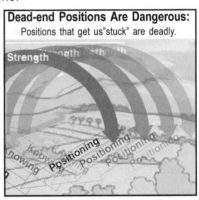

Dead-end Positions Are Dangerous:
Positions that get us"stuck" are deadly.

Sun Tzu's teaches us to be deeply suspicious of every new area into which we venture. If a given market, organization, or situation can hide oppositions, we must actively seek it out. We cannot compete unless with know where the opposition is. We are taught to hide our own positions and movements, so we must suspect that opposition is hiding their positions and movements from us.

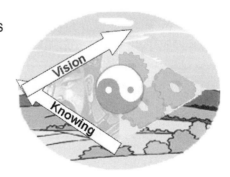

Sometimes, the enemy is close by but remains calm.
Expect to find him in a natural stronghold.
Other times, he remains at a distance but provokes battle.
He wants you to attack him.

He sometimes shifts the position of his camp.
He is looking for an advantageous position.

The trees in the forest move.
Expect that the enemy is coming.
The tall grasses obstruct your view.
Be suspicious.

The birds take flight.
Expect that the enemy is hiding.
Animals startle.
Expect an ambush.

Notice the dust.
It sometimes rises high in a straight line.
Vehicles are coming.
The dust appears low in a wide band.
Foot soldiers are coming.
The dust seems scattered in different areas.
The enemy is collecting firewood.
Any dust is light and settling down.
The enemy is setting up camp.

At this point, Sun Tzu tells us how to evaluate competitive behavior as we move into a new competitive arena. In general, we can summarize this advice as ignoring an opponent's words but watching and interpreting their every action carefully.

When competitors change their approach, it means that they've seen an opportunity or discovered a weakness.

We often can't see our oppositions' moves directly, but we can infer them from what we see in the business environment, among suppliers and customers. If we can't get good information from these sources, we must be suspicious.

We can know when the opposition is planning a surprise by the way our business contacts act. If they know something about the competition that they are suppose to keep a secret, they will act suspiciously.

We can put together a picture of competitive action from the smallest amounts of information. We can have an idea about what opponents are doing by the amount of evidence we find, the places we find it, and by seeing if it is increasing or decreasing. We have to continually

An Enemy Model
We must use the signs in the environment to create a complete picture of our situation.

monitor even the smallest rumors about competitive activity to put together a meaningful picture.

Your enemy speaks humbly while building up forces.
He is planning to advance.

The enemy talks aggressively and pushes as if to advance.
He is planning to retreat.

Small vehicles exit his camp first and move to positions on
the army's flanks.
They are forming a battle line.

Your enemy tries to sue for peace but without offering a
treaty.
He is plotting.

Your enemy's men run to leave and yet form ranks.
You should expect action.

Half his army advances and the other half retreats.
He is luring you.

Your enemy plans to fight but his men just stand there.
They are starving.

Those who draw water drink it first.
They are thirsty.

Your enemy sees an advantage but does not advance.
His men are tired.

Birds gather.
Your enemy has abandoned his camp.

Here, the advice is to believe the opposite of what the opponents say. If they talk weak, they are probably strong.

For this reason, we shouldn't fear aggressive behavior; it is often a smoke screen for weakness.

Since we generally want to avoid direct confrontations, we should be sensitive to any indication that our opponents are planning to put up a fight.

However, this doesn't mean that we should trust competitors who want to call a truce without being specific. We want to avoid confrontations, but we must distrust vagueness.

We must expect that opponents will also mislead with actions as well as words, feigning one move while planning another.

We must suspect what looks like obvious confusion on the part of our opponents.

We can also judge opponents by their associates.

People act out of their *individual* self-interest first.

Individual Action or Group Plan?

If people are acting strangely, it is because their organization is no longer satisfying their needs.

When a competitor abandons a given position, it creates a flurry of activity in the environment.

Your enemy's soldiers call in the night.
They are afraid.

Your enemy's army is raucous.
They do not take their commander seriously.

Your enemy's banners and flags shift.
Order is breaking down.

Your enemy's officers are irritable.
They are exhausted.

Your enemy's men kill their horses for meat.
They are out of provisions.

They don't put their pots away or return to their tents.
They expect to fight to the death.

Enemy troops appear sincere and agreeable.
But their men are slow to speak to each other.
They are no longer united.

Your enemy offers too many incentives to his men.
He is in trouble.

Your enemy gives out too many punishments.
His men are weary.

Your enemy first attacks and then is afraid of your larger
force.
His best troops have not arrived.

Again, people act out of individual self-interest. If an opponent's people are contacting us, they are worried about their jobs.

When we hear a competitor's people complaining about their management, we know their leadership is not respected.

Reorganizations are another sign of internal friction, fractures, and breakdown of unity and focus.

We shouldn't interpret middle management hostility as aimed at us. But rather view it as frustration with their organization.

When we see competitors selling off their assets for cash, we must assume that they are running low on resources.

When our competition is really in bad shape, however, they can become more dangerous.

Though these warnings are all phrased in English as ways of evaluating our enemy, the original Chinese is ambiguous. They can also be warnings about evaluating our organization.

Sun Tzu teaches that we motivate groups by self-interest, but if we have to bribe people, they aren't truly part of the group.

Sun Tzu believes in strong discipline, especially for new people, but overusing discipline is just laziness.

Speed is a central factor in war. This means that our enemies may sometimes attack before they are ready. We must be wary that this is just a stalling tactic, not a true mistake.

Your enemy comes in a conciliatory manner.
He needs to rest and recuperate.

Your enemy is angry and appears to welcome battle.
This goes on for a long time, but he doesn't attack.
He also doesn't leave the field.
You must watch him carefully.

If you are too weak to fight, you must find more men.
In this situation, you must not act aggressively.
You must unite your forces, expect the enemy, recruit men
and wait.

You must be cautious about making plans and adjust to the
enemy.
You must increase the size of your forces.

With new, undedicated soldiers, you can depend on them if
you discipline them.
They will tend to disobey your orders.
If they do not obey your orders, they will be useless.

You can depend on seasoned, dedicated soldiers.
But you must avoid disciplining them without reason.
Otherwise, you cannot use them.

You must control your soldiers with *esprit de corp*.
You must bring them together by winning victories.
You must get them to believe in you.

If fighting when you're not ready can be a delaying tactic, pretending to be making peace can certainly be one also.

Sometimes an opponent's behavior is just confusing. Do they want a direct confrontation or not? In these cases, Sun Tzu advises that we avoid initiating any action. We must wait and see what the competition does.

ð—☆

When we expand into new areas, we have to know when to stop. At some point, our human resources are stretched too thin to expand. If we don't have more resources than we need to continue expansion, we must stop and get more people.

Notice how Sun Tzu makes competitive expansion about people. Moving into new areas requires trained people, not just money or other resources. Competition demands people.

ð—☆

If competitive expansion requires trained people, how do we bring them into the organization? Sun Tzu makes it clear that we must demand a lot from our new people. We make it clear up front that we are going to challenge them.

We must take a very different approach in managing our seasoned employees. If we are tough on new people, we must give our seasoned people a great deal of freedom.

People truly become part of our organizations when we have won successes together. People identify with an organization once they have contributed to its success.

Make it easy for them to obey your orders by training your people.
Your people will then obey you.
If you do not make it easy to obey, you won't train your people.
Then they will not obey.

Make your commands easy to follow.
You must understand the way a crowd thinks.

This chapter started with moving into new areas, but it closes by emphasizing the need to train our people. In Sun Tzu's system, everyone in the organization must have a thorough grounding in the organization's philosophy. This is the source of unity and focus. We must make it easy for people to understand our organization's purpose and their role in it.

To bring our people together, we must understand group psychology and how to create shared success.

Train People to Focus Them
Sun Tzu teaches that focus comes from a shared philosophy where everyone sees his or her individual self-interest served by working together.

FIELD POSITION

Some field positions are unobstructed.
Some field positions are entangling.
Some field positions are supporting.
Some field positions are constricted.
Some field positions give you a barricade.
Some field positions are spread out.

You can attack from some positions easily.
Others can attack you easily as well.
We call these unobstructed positions.
These positions are open.
On them, be the first to occupy a high, sunny area.
Put yourself where you can defend your supply routes.
Then you will have an advantage.

The easiest way to understand this chapter is to think of Sun Tzu's "six field positions" as dimensions on a pyramid. Pairs of "field positions" form a range of characteristics that define a plane on this pyramid.

The Opportunity Pyramid
A matrix for evaluating positions.

The first side of this pyramid is the dimension Sun Tzu calls "obstacle." The broad or common description of opportunities on this dimension is "unobstructed." We show this characteristic at the base of our pyramid. Unobstructed opportunities are generally good but no better for us than they are for the competition. Our major concern in managing them is caring for our source of supply since there is a danger of outdistancing our supplies in these unobstructed situations.

The Obstacle Plane
Unobstructed Positions at the bottom.

You can attack from some positions easily.
Disaster arises when you try to return to them.
These are entangling positions.
These field positions are one-sided.
Wait until your enemy is unprepared.
You can then attack from these positions and win.
Avoid a well prepared enemy.
You will try to attack and lose.
Since you can't return, you will meet disaster.
These field positions offer no advantage.

I cannot leave some positions without losing an advantage.
If the enemy leaves this ground, he also loses an advantage.
We call these supporting field positions.
These positions strengthen you.
The enemy may try to entice me away.
Still, I will hold my position.
You must entice the enemy to leave.
You then strike him as he is leaving.
These field positions offer an advantage.

Some field positions are constricted.
I try to get to these positions before the enemy does.
You must fill these areas and await the enemy.
Sometimes, the enemy will reach them first.
If he fills them, do not follow him.
But if he fails to fill them, you can go after him.

The next dimension is a kind of stickiness that Sun Tzu calls "danger." Its broad, common characteristic is "being entangling." These are positions or opportunities that trap you: you can leave them but not go back. In business, we see this all the time. For example, if a business that sells through distributors starts selling directly to customers, they will find it very difficult or impossible to go back to distribution if their direct sales approach doesn't work.

The Danger Plane
Positions that trap us.

The narrow or uncommon characteristic on the "stickiness" plane is "being supportive." We show it at the top of our pyramid. We are still stuck in a supportive position, but the position is so good and has such a good future that we don't want to leave it. There is no line separating supportive and entangling positions. The difference is simply the amount of promise and future that the position has.

The next plan is "distance." Its narrow or rare characteristic is "being constricted." Distance gauges how broadly or narrowly we are spread out. In Sun Tzu's system, constricted opportunities are very good if we are willing to concentrate on them and "fill them up" or satisfy them completely. Being constricted perfectly defines the top of any pyramid.

The Distance Plane
Are we united?

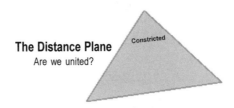

Some field positions give you a barricade.
I get to these positions before the enemy does.
You occupy their southern, sunny heights and wait for the
enemy.
Sometimes the enemy occupies these areas first.
If so, entice him away.
Never go after him.

Some field positions are too spread out.
Your force may seem equal to the enemy.
Still you will lose if you provoke a battle.
If you fight, you will not have any advantage.

These are the six types of field positions.
Each battleground has its own rules.
As a commander, you must know where to go.
You must examine each position closely.

Some armies can be outmaneuvered.
Some armies are too lax.
Some armies fall down.
Some armies fall apart.
Some armies are disorganized.
Some armies must retreat.

Know all six of these weaknesses.
They lead to losses on both good and bad ground.
They all arise from the army's commander.

92

"Barricaded" is the narrow dimension of the "obstacle" plane that we began with. The opposite of being unobstructed, these positions are also very positive. This plane is the only "all positive" plane, but obstructed positions, being at the top of the pyramid are rarer and more desirable than unobstructed positions are.

All Good
The obstacles plane.

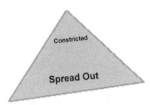

The last, broad and very negative characteristic of the "distance" dimension is "being spread out."

Positions are stepping stones to better positions. We want to move from bottom, unobstructed positions to the narrow top of the pyramid

The Natural and Best Path
Start low in unobstructed positions and move up to "higher" positions.

Notice how the six weaknesses in armies coincide with the six types of positions. Though Sun Tzu makes it clear that they don't come from the ground, these problems tend to show up when trying to take advantage of different types of opportunities, which is why he explores them here.

Sun Tzu always attributes every weakness of any army to poor command. People are people and never the problem. We choose the positions that we put our people into. It all comes down to management to choose the right positions and train people properly.

One general can command a force equal to the enemy.
Still his enemy outflanks him.
This means that his army can be outmaneuvered.

Another can have strong soldiers, but weak officers.
This means that his army will be too lax.

Another has strong officers but weak soldiers.
This means that his army will fall down.

Another has sub-commanders that are angry and defiant.
They attack the enemy and fight their own battles.
As a commander, he cannot know the battlefield.
This means that his army will fall apart.

Another general is weak and easygoing.
He fails to make his orders clear.
His officers and men lack direction,
This shows in his military formations.
This means that his army will be disorganized.

Another general fails to predict the enemy.
He pits his small forces against larger ones.
He puts his weak forces against stronger ones.
He fails to pick his fights correctly.
This means that his army must retreat.

You must know all about these six weaknesses.
You must understand the philosophies that lead to defeat.
When a general arrives, you can know what he will do.
You must study each one carefully.

94

Problems with being outmaneuvered show on an unobstructed terrain. When both our opponents and we can move easily, we must not be outmaneuvered.

The challenge of entangling terrain is to wait until the time is right to attack. A lax organization lacks the discipline to do this.

Supportive terrain makes survival easy, but the organization will fall down if it is ever challenged.

Constricted terrain demands focus. If the organization isn't united, it can't maintain a focus. This focus demands the attention and commitment of every level of the organization. Without it, the organization falls apart.

A leader's easygoing nature is most likely to become a problem in barricaded situations when the leader feels safe and secure.

Our forces are weaker than the competition's when we spread out. When we spread out we fail to predict opposing action.

The Weaknesses of Organizations
Directly related to the six "field positions."

Any of the six weaknesses of a leader can appear in any situation, but they are most likely to become a problem in dealing with certain types of opportunities. For a given type of opportunity, we can predict who is more suited to succeed if we understand these weaknesses.

You must control your field position.
It will always strengthen your army.

You must predict the enemy to overpower him and win.
You must analyze the obstacles, dangers, and distances.
This is the best way to command.

Understand your field position before you go to battle.
Then you will win.
You can fail to understand your field position and still fight.
Then you will lose.

You must provoke battle when you will certainly win.
It doesn't matter what you are ordered.
The government may order you not to fight.
Despite that, you must always fight when you will win.

Sometimes provoking a battle will lead to a loss.
The government may order you to fight.
Despite that, you must avoid battle when you will lose.

You must advance without desiring praise.
You must retreat without fearing shame.
The only correct move is to preserve your troops.
This is how you serve your country.
This is how you reward your nation.

A fundamental principle of Sun Tzu's system is that success means choosing the right opportunity.

We must know how to analyze any opportunity in a dynamic environment. What is its character?

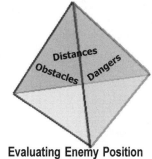

In this stanza, "going to battle" is best understood as choosing a given opportunity. We must pick the right opportunities to succeed.

Evaluating Enemy Position
Does the opportunity fit the organization?

What is the major obstacle to being opportunistic? The "productive" parts of our organization (the "nation" in *Sun Tzu*) want predictable, "planned" opportunities, while the competitive side wants opportunities it can win.

In this conflict between the two halves of the organization, Sun Tzu says we must follow our competitive impulse. We must go after what we can win and ignore what is "planned."

Here, Sun Tzu makes it clear that this battle for leadership in the organization cannot be a mater of ego.
It is a matter of success and survival.

Avoiding Battles for Leadership
Competitive and productive roles must support each other.

Think of your soldiers as little children.
You can make them follow you into a deep river.
Treat them as your beloved children.
You can lead them all to their deaths.

Some leaders are generous, but cannot use their men.
They love their men, but cannot command them.
Their men are unruly and disorganized.
These leaders create spoiled children.
Their soldiers are useless.

You may know what your soldiers will do in an attack.
You may not know if the enemy is vulnerable to attack.
You will then win only half the time.
You may know that the enemy is vulnerable to attack.
You may not know if your men are capable of attacking them.
You will still win only half the time.
You may know that the enemy is vulnerable to attack.
You may know that your men are ready to attack.
You may not know how to position yourself in the field for battle.
You will still win only half the time.

You must know how to make war.
You can then act without confusion.
You can attempt anything.

Moving into new opportunities requires the support of *all* our people. For Sun Tzu, this means having the right unifying philosophy.

Unity from Philosophy

Good philosophy is more complicated than simply treating people well. As you can see from looking at organizational weaknesses, many come from poor discipline, weak management, and poor communication. Good discipline, management, and communication are critical.

Here, Sun Tzu reminds us that we now have two ways of evaluating our competitive situation. We have the "Five Element Model," which we use to analyze our organization and our opponents. To this we have added the "Opportunity Pyramid," which we can use to analyze our opportunities and our relative fit with these opportunities in comparison to the fit of our potential opponents.

Two Models
For analysing ourselves, opponents, and positions.

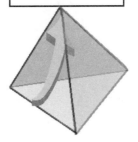

The purpose of mastering these two devices is to enable us to choose our opportunities without hesitation.

We say:
Know the enemy and know yourself.
Your victory will be painless.
Know the weather and the field.
Your victory will be complete.

❖

We must use these two devices together to understand our complete situation. We must first know our relative strengths versus those of the competition. We must then know how a given opportunity in a particular time and place suits our particular abilities.

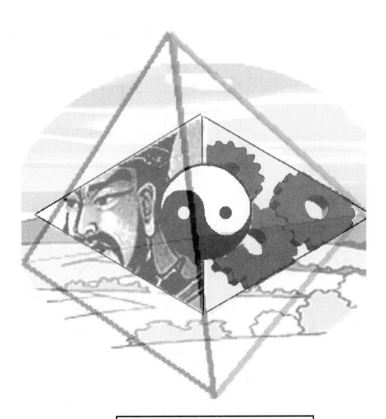

Positions within Positions
We evaluate our opportunities to choose the
right position in the environment

TYPES OF TERRAIN

Use the art of war.
Know when the terrain will scatter you.
Know when the terrain will be easy.
Know when the terrain will be disputed.
Know when the terrain is open.
Know when the terrain is intersecting.
Know when the terrain is dangerous.
Know when the terrain is bad.
Know when the terrain is confined.
Know when the terrain is deadly.

Warring parties must sometimes fight inside their own
territory.
This is scattering terrain.

When you enter hostile territory, your penetration is shallow.
This is easy terrain.

Some terrain gives me an advantageous position.
However, it gives others an advantageous position as well.
This will be disputed terrain.

THE AMAZING SECRETS OF CAMPAIGN STAGES

In this chapter, we look at the basic action needed in the various conditions or stages that any competitive project passes through. Not every campaign will go through all of the stages,

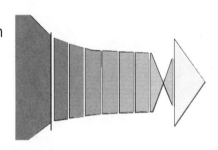

but we should always be prepared for each of them. If we can recognize them, we will know how to react properly.

First, we can begin a campaign defending within our own territory. These are situations which tend to "scatter" or disburse our support.

Beginning in a new area is often unopposed and goes very easily.

We enter into another stage when we go after an area that is too obviously desirable. The competition makes that area profitable for no one.

I can use some terrain to advance easily.
Others can advance along with us.
This is open terrain.

Everyone shares access to a given area.
The first one there can gather a larger group than anyone
else.
This is intersecting terrain.

You can penetrate deeply into hostile territory.
Then many hostile cities are behind you.
This is dangerous terrain.

There are mountain forests.
There are rugged hills.
There are marshes.
Everyone confronts these obstacles on a campaign.
They make bad terrain.

In some areas, the passage is narrow.
You are closed in as you enter and exit them.
In this type of area, a few people can attack our much larger
force.
This is confined terrain.

You can sometimes survive only if you fight quickly.
You will die if you delay.
This is deadly terrain.

These are the three "middle" stages. The best of them is the "open" situation, which Sun Tzu describes as a race between the opponents and us.

In many campaigns or projects, we cannot deliver a complete "product" ourselves. We need to find other organizations that we can join with to complete that stage or product.

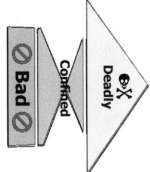

This is a late, middle-stage problem. We are deeply invested in a campaign and our "supply lines" are cut off by the opposition (sometimes from within our own organization).

This brings us to the three late stages. The first of these is the "bad" stage. Many campaigns and projects meet difficult times toward their end. This is especially true in sales campaigns where customer resistance increases toward the end of the sale when a decision has to be made.

Another common end-stage situation is the "confined" situation, which is a situation where only a few people are critical to our success. These are often transitional stages when only a few people understand the new system.

This is the simplest and most straightforward end-stage situation. Here, we must act quickly.

To be successful, you control scattering terrain by not
fighting.
Control easy terrain by not stopping.
Control disputed terrain by not attacking.
Control open terrain by staying with the enemy's forces.
Control intersecting terrain by uniting with your allies.
Control dangerous terrain by plundering.
Control bad terrain by keeping on the move.
Control confined terrain by using surprise.
Control deadly terrain by fighting.

Go to any area that helps you in waging war.
You use it to cut off the enemy's contact between his front
and back lines.
Prevent his small parties from relying on his larger force.
Stop his strong divisions from rescuing his weak ones.
Prevent his officers from getting his men together.
Chase his soldiers apart to stop them from amassing.
Harass them to prevent their ranks from forming.

When joining battle gives you an advantage, you must do it.
When it isn't to your benefit, you must avoid it.

A daring soldier may ask:
"A large, organized enemy army and its general are coming.
What do I do to prepare for them?"

The correct action required at each of these stages is simple. In the early stages, we must avoid making the wrong but often natural move. In the middle stages, we maintain the pressure. In the later stages, we have to finish the process. The beginning prescription is the exact opposite of the ending prescription.

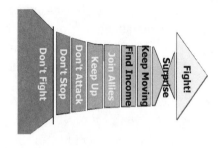

The lesson in dividing the enemy addresses the issue of scattering territory. We don't want our opponents to attack us on our own ground. Instead, we want to take the battle to them. When we do, we put them on scattering ground. Attacking on their ground means forcing them to address our issues, losing their focus and breaking their uniting philosophy.

If we are attacked on our own ground, we must avoid the battle.

The question is, how do we avoid the battle when an able opponent is coming into our territory? The basic prescription of "don't fight" is more difficult than it seems.

Tell him:
"First seize an area that the enemy must have.
Then they will pay attention to you.
Mastering speed is the essence of war.
Take advantage of a large enemy's inability to keep up.
Use a philosophy of avoiding difficult situations.
Attack the area where he doesn't expect you."

You must use the philosophy of an invader.
Invade deeply and then concentrate your forces.
This controls your men without oppressing them.

Get your supplies from the riches of the territory.
It is sufficient to supply your whole army.

Take care of your men and do not overtax them.
Your *esprit de corps* increases your momentum.
Keep your army moving and plan for surprises.
Make it difficult for the enemy to count your forces.
Position your men where there is no place to run.
They will then face death without fleeing.
They will find a way to survive.
Your officers and men will fight to their utmost.

Military officers that are completely committed lose their fear.
When they have nowhere to run, they must stand firm.
Deep in enemy territory, they are captives.
Since they cannot escape, they will fight.

We prevent opponents from coming into our area by quickly taking the battle to them. When Sun Tzu says that we want our opponents to "pay attention to us", he means that they will then have to deal with our advance into their territory instead of advancing into ours. This type of preemptive strike isn't a true advance. We don't actually want to confront our opponents, so we must be quick and evasive with preemptive attacks.

The essence of expansion in competitive campaigns is going into the territory of others. In these areas, our people are the outsiders. This brings them together.

We want these campaigns to be self-financing as soon as possible. We cannot support them by continued investment.

The point of all earlier stages is to bring our people to a "do-or-die" conclusion. The earlier stages of invasion are meant only to take us to the final one. At the final stages, our people must be completely dependent on the success of the campaign.

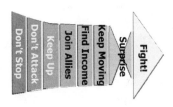

Once people are completely committed to the project, they will find a way to make it work. Sun Tzu describes them as captives in the opponent's territory, but this also means that they are free of the "mother" organization, free to control their future.

Commit your men completely.
Without being posted, they will be on guard.
Without being asked, they will get what is needed.
Without being forced, they will be dedicated.
Without being given orders, they can be trusted.

Stop them from guessing by removing all their doubts.
Stop them from dying by giving them no place to run.

Your officers may not be rich.
Nevertheless, they still desire plunder.
They may die young.
Nevertheless, they still want to live forever.

You must order the time of attack.
Officers and men may sit and weep until their lapels are wet.
When they stand up, tears may stream down their cheeks.
Put them in a position where they cannot run.
They will show the greatest courage under fire.

Make good use of war.
This demands instant reflexes.
You must develop these instant reflexes.
Act like an ordinary mountain snake.
Someone can strike at your head.
You can then attack with your tail
Someone can strike at your tail.
You can then attack with your head.
Someone can strike at your middle.
You can then attack with both your head and tail.

Sun Tzu has a tremendous faith in the strength and intelligence of individuals when their self-interest is on the line. When people are completely committed to a cause (and dependent on its success), they don't have to be managed. They are capable of managing themselves.

The secret to giving them this independence is keeping them completely informed about *their* situation (not our plans).

All individuals have an entrepreneur inside them. Every mid-level manager wants to be a tycoon. People will take risks to be successful because they desire more than what they have.

When we challenge our people, they can rise to extraordinary heights. They can be afraid or uncertain, but our strong direction puts them in a position to succeed.

As we move from one competitive stage to another, our entire organization must instantly recognize our situation and react appropriately. Ignorance and poor communication prevent different parts of the organization from supporting the other. A favorite topic of Sun Tzu's is how easily organizations are fragmented. In competitive situations, every part of our organization must be able to *independently* synchronize their reactions based upon their shared philosophy, shared understanding of appropriate behavior, *and* shared knowledge of their situation.

A daring soldier asks:
"Can any army imitate these instant reflexes?"
We answer:
"It can."

To command and get the most of proud people, you must
study adversity.
People work together when they are in the same boat during
a storm.
In this situation, one rescues the other just as the right hand
helps the left.

Use adversity correctly.
Tether your horses and bury your wagon's wheels.
Still, you can't depend on this alone.
An organized force is braver than lone individuals.
This is the art of organization.
Put the tough and weak together.
You must also use the terrain.

Make good use of war.
Unite your men as one.
Never let them give up.

The commander must be a military professional.
This requires confidence and detachment.
You must maintain dignity and order.
You must control what your men see and hear.
They must follow you without knowing your plans.

Many "leaders" don't trust the ability of their people to make independent decisions correctly and quickly. We must train our people so that we can depend upon their reactions if we are to be successful.

To get people to work together, we must put them in situations where their success depends on the success of the organization as a whole. They shouldn't be able to be "successful" in their job if the organization fails.

Adversity and problems can and should unite a well-managed organization. Our people must see how that working together minimizes their weaknesses and leverages their strengths.

Many stages in a competitive campaign are bad, dangerous, and even deadly—to use Sun Tzu's terms—but they can draw people together and strengthen them if we manage them well.

Leaders are separate from the organization. As a leader, we cannot be "just one of the guys." People want and need to look up to and respect their leaders. This means that we must act in a way that inspires devotion. We must manage everything that we do and say considering its emotional effect on people.

113

You can reinvent your men's roles.
You can change your plans.
You can use your men without their understanding.

You must shift your campgrounds.
You must take detours from the ordinary routes.
You must use your men without giving them your strategy.

A commander provides what his army needs now.
You must be willing to climb high and then kick away your
ladder.
You must be able to lead your men deeply into your enemy's
territory and then find a way to create the opportunity that
you need.

You must drive men like a flock of sheep.

You must drive them to march.
You must drive them to attack.
You must never let them know where you are headed.
You must unite them into a great army.
You must then drive them against all opposition.
This is the job of a true commander.

You must adapt to the different terrain.
You must adapt to find an advantage.
You must manage your people's affections.
You must study all these skills.

The "without their understanding" here is misleading. The point is that if people understand the shared goal and shared danger, they aren't tied to the specifics of a job or a plan.

People who are habituated to their job lose sight of the shared goal. We must continually change our methods so that people don't lose sight of the external competitive realities.

The leader's vision must provide the necessary challenges for their people. In moving people into challenging situations, we are putting them in a position to succeed.

Think, "challenge" here, and not slave driving.

Don't take this message incorrectly. Sun Tzu does not believe in pushing people beyond their endurance. In chapter seven, he specifically warns about how "hurry" destroys unity. What he means here is that we must challenge people, keep them busy, and keep them moving. If people are constantly challenged, they develop the habit of overcoming obstacles.

Remember, what Sun Tzu calls different "terrains" is really more like different stages through which we have to move. When he says, "adapt," he means we must suit our behavior to the situation, so we *must* know the right behavior for this situation.

Always use the philosophy of invasion.
Deep invasions concentrate your forces.
Shallow invasions scatter your forces.
When you leave your country and cross the border, you must
take control.
This is always critical ground.
You can sometimes move in any direction.
This is always intersecting ground.
You can penetrate deeply into a territory.
This is always dangerous ground.
You penetrate only a little way.
This is always easy ground.
Your retreat is closed and the path ahead tight.
This is always confined ground.
There is sometimes no place to run.
This is always deadly ground.

To use scattering terrain correctly, we must inspire our men's
devotion.
On easy terrain, we must keep in close communication.
On disputed terrain, we should try to hamper the enemy's
progress.
On open terrain, we must carefully defend our chosen
position.
On intersecting terrain, we must solidify our alliances.
On dangerous terrain, we must ensure our food supplies.
On bad terrain, we must keep advancing along the road.
On confined terrain, we must make block flow from our
headquarters.
On deadly terrain, we must show what we can do by killing
the enemy.

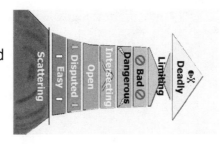

We describe these "terrains" as stages because Sun Tzu clearly meant for us to see a competitive campaign as a process. A process has a clear beginning, middle, and end. The beginning must be a "philosophy of invasion," that is, competition by taking the battle to the enemy instead of waiting for an attack. This is a philosophy of expansion and growth. In this expansion, certain situations are likely to occur. At first, progress is easy. At the end, it gets difficult. If it turns out that you can share needs and interests with other organizations, you can use partners. You may squeeze through difficult transitions. In the end, however, it always comes down to the need to do or die.

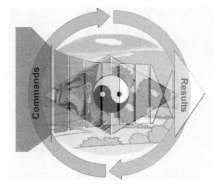

At each stage, we have to continually manage the emotional well being of our people. Again in chapter seven, Sun Tzu told us the emotional content of our commands is the most important part of our message to our people. Food is important because it sends a message. Competitive campaigns are won and lost on the emotional attitudes of the people involved. We alone must control the flow of information through the organization.

Make your men feel like an army.
Surround them and they will defend themselves.
If they cannot avoid it, they will fight.
If they are under pressure, they will obey.

Do the right thing when you don't know your different
enemies' plans.
Don't attempt to meet them.

You don't know the local mountains, forests, hills and
marshes?
Then you cannot march the army.
You don't have local guides?
You won't get any of the benefits of the terrain.

There are many factors in war.
You may lack knowledge of any one of them.
If so, it is wrong to take a nation into war.

You must be able to dominate a nation at war.
Divide a big nation before they are able to gather a large
force.
Increase your enemy's fear.
Prevent his forces from getting together and organizing.

Do the right thing and don't try to compete for outside
alliances.
You won't have to fight for authority.
Trust only yourself and your own resources.
This increases the enemy's uncertainty.
You can force one of his allies to pull out.
His whole nation can fall.

In the end, we win the dedication of our people by putting them in situations where they can win and, just as importantly, *must* win. If we leave people an "out", we are inviting failure. Instead, we must demand their total commitment.

Here, Sun Tzu puts the Nine Stages into the larger context of the Four Skills. To be successful in a campaign, we must have vision, that is, see the opening left by the enemy.

The foundation of this vision is knowledge of the territory. We cannot see an opportunity worthy of a campaign unless we have a deep understanding of the area into which we want to move.

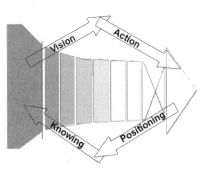

A successful campaign takes us to a new position and a new stepping stone.

Today, we call this process of dividing up the competitive landscape segmenting the market. We pick a small area to focus on, attacking what is poorly defending, dividing the competition.

Sun Tzu is deeply suspicious of alliances that don't happen naturally, that is, those for which we have to compete. Though everything is a competition, unity is so important and so difficult between organizations that alliances are all suspect. Add to this the idea that large organizations are inherently slower than small ones, and alliances become even more difficult to justify. Sun Tzu would rather make war on alliances than depend on them.

119

Distribute plunder without worrying about agreements.
Halt without the government's command.
Attack with the whole strength of your army.
Use your army as if it was a single man.

Attack with skill.
Do not discuss it.
Attack when you have an advantage.
Do not talk about the dangers.
When you can launch your army into deadly ground, even if
it stumbles, it can still survive.
You can be weakened in a deadly battle and yet be stronger
afterward.

Even a large force can fall into misfortune.
If you fall behind, however, you can still turn defeat into
victory.
You must use the skills of war.
To survive, you must adapt to your enemy's purpose.
You must stay with him no matter where he goes.
It may take a thousand miles to kill the general.
If you correctly understand him, you can find the skill to do
it.

Manage your government correctly at the start of a war.
Close your borders and tear up passports.
Block the passage of envoys.
Encourage politicians at headquarters to stay out of it.
You must use any means to put an end to politics.
Your enemy's people will leave you an opening.
You must instantly invade through it.

The most important advantage of working outside alliances is that you don't have to deal with the politics of larger organizations. The freer the competitive unit is to work toward its own ends, the more united and strong it is.

Using Sun Tzu's methods, we go into every situation planning, positioning, and acting to win. We only go into campaigns that we *know* we can win, that is, where we have a clear advantage. At the same time, however, we are also aware that loss is always a possibility. We don't talk about this with our people. We never act as though failure is an option. Still, we know that success and failure go in cycles.

The larger reality is that, especially when it comes to explorations into new areas, failure is possible, even likely. However, failing the right way can still allow us to make good progress toward eventual, certain success.

At the end of this long and detailed chapter, Sun Tzu takes a step back and looks at the big picture. When we plan to undertake a competitive campaign, we must know what we are doing. First, we must get control of information and make sure that the competitive part of the organization is in firm control. We then wait to see an opening. When we see that opening, the competitive campaign begins.

Immediately seize a place that they love.
Do it quickly.
Trample any border to pursue the enemy.
Use your judgment about when to fight.

Doing the right thing at the start of war is like approaching a
woman.
Your enemy's men must open the door.
After that, you should act like a streaking rabbit.
The enemy will be unable to catch you.

A successful competitive campaign depends totally on fighting our battles on our competitor's ground. We must act quickly to segment the market or trample a border. We must look for support from the trends of the moment.

Even though Sun Tzu provides a very complete, detailed vision about how competitive systems work, he clearly teaches the art of war as well as the science of war. Using his system demands the subtlety and sensitivity of a man wooing a woman. It also demands pure speed.

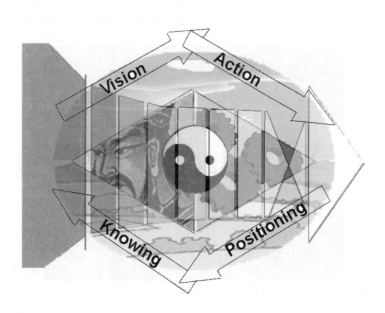

Attacking with Fire

There are five ways of attacking with fire.
The first is burning troops.
The second is burning supplies.
The third is burning supply transport.
The fourth is burning storehouses.
The fifth is burning camps.

To make fire, you must have the resources.
To build a fire, you must prepare the raw materials.

To attack with fire, you must be in the right season.
To start a fire, you must have the time.

Choose the right season.
The weather must be very dry.

Choose the right time.
Pick a season when the grass is as high as the side of a cart.

You can tell the proper days by the stars in the night sky.
You want days when the wind rises in the morning.

THE AMAZING SECRETS OF USING THE ENVIRONMENT

This chapter gives us the general rules for using weapons, more specifically, *environmental* weapons. In Sun Tzu's time, the primary way a competitor could leverage the environment against the opponent was by using fire. In the business competition of our time, we can use the press, the legal system, and even the financial system against our competitors.

To use this type of attack on the competition, the environment must provide the raw materials.

This attack is highly dependent on having an opportunity.

Think of bad publicity, lawsuits, and buyouts as having a season.

We cannot create the fuel for these attacks; we must discover it.

We can, however, choose the timing for this type of attack. We must choose a time when social forces will support it.

Everyone attacks with fire.
You must create five different situations with fire and be able
to adjust to them.

You start a fire inside the enemy's camp.
Then attack the enemy's periphery.

You launch a fire attack, but the enemy remains calm.
Wait and do not attack.

The fire reaches its height.
Follow its path if you can.
If you can't follow it, stay where you are.

Spreading fires on the outside of camp can kill.
You can't always get fire inside the enemy's camp.
Take your time in spreading it.

Set the fire when the wind is at your back.
Don't attack into the wind.
Daytime winds last a long time.
Night winds fade quickly.

Every army must know how to deal with the five attacks by
fire.
Use many men to guard against them.

This means that we must be prepared to defend against these types of attacks as well as use them. We must be prepared to defend against bad publicity, lawsuits, financial pressure, etc.

Moving against opponents when their people are in disarray is the first and most common way to use an environmental attack.

If the target doesn't panic, the second approach is simply to wait for the "fire" to do its damage without attacking directly.

Environmental fires build and fade with time. When the heat of the "fire" fades, we can move against the weaknesses that it creates in our opponent.

The fourth situation is an indirect attack. An environmental attack may not damage an opponent's organization directly, but it can still weaken their position in the marketplace.

The fifth situation is to leverage the trends in the environment. If sexual lawsuits or news stories are popular at the time, they become likely attacks. If the current hot topic is "windfall profits," that is where the danger is. Visibility (daytime) is the key here.

We must constantly be evaluating the environment and current information to identify the opportunities for these attacks. We look for opportunities to attack as well as situations where we might need to defend.

**Evaluate Opportunity
and Danger**
For environmental attacks

The
Leader's
Job

Vision

127

When you use fire to assist your attacks, you are being
clever.
Water can add force to an attack.
You can also use water to disrupt an enemy.
It doesn't, however, take his resources.

You win in battle by getting the opportunity to attack.
It is dangerous if you fail to study how to accomplish this
achievement.
As commander, you cannot waste your opportunities.

We say:
A wise leader plans success.
A good general studies it.
If there is little to be gained, don't act.
If there is little to win, do not use your men.
If there is no danger, don't fight.

As leader, you cannot let your anger interfere with the
success of your forces.
As commander, you cannot fight simply because you are
enraged.
Join the battle only when it is in your advantage to act.
If there is no advantage in joining a battle, stay put.

Anger can change back into happiness.
Rage can change back into joy.
A nation once destroyed cannot be brought back to life.
Dead men do not return to the living.

Here, Sun Tzu contrasts attacks where we put the "heat" on our opponents with another type of environmental attack. Water is Sun Tzu's metaphor for change. Technological change is also an environmental weapon, but though it puts pressure on opponents, it doesn't damage them like "fire" attacks.

Many people are uncomfortable using these types of environmental attacks against the opposition. However, like all opportunities that we are given, we must make the most of what we have. We cannot afford to disregard them.

These attacks (and all competitive attacks) require the proper foresight and deliberation on the part of a leader. They should be not used lightly. Remember the lessons of chapter two: attacking is always costly; even these "fire" attacks have costs. We must make sure that we have something real to gain before we undertake them. Victory is making winning pay!

Earlier in this chapter, Sun Tzu points out that the secret to defending against environmental attacks—bad press, law suits, buyout threats, etc.—is to keep calm. Here he extends that advice to make it clear that we should never launch any attack because of our emotions.

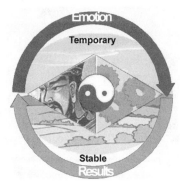

In Sun Tzu's system, emotions are fleeting, belonging to the realm of heaven, but we have to live with the results of emotion on the hard, solid ground of reality.

Control Emotions to Control Results

This fact must make a wise leader cautious.
A good general is on guard.

Your philosophy must be to keep the nation peaceful and the army intact.

We cannot be too sensitive to use these attacks, we never use them out of anger, and we must always defend against them.

These attacks must be productive in the sense of enriching us so that we preserve and build our competitive ability.

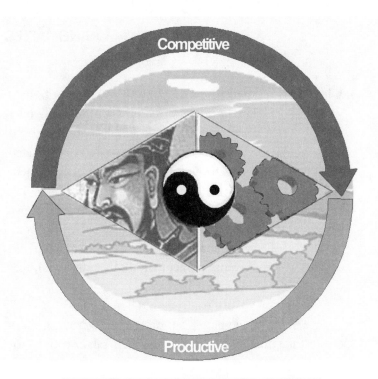

The Twin Dangers of Environmental Attacks
We must protect both our competitive and productive abilities in preventing and fighting these "fires."

USING SPIES

Altogether, building an army requires thousands of men.
They invade and march thousands of miles.
Whole families are destroyed.
Other families must be heavily taxed.
Every day, thousands of dollars must be spent.

Internal and external events force people to move.
They are unable to work while on the road.
They are unable to find and hold a useful job.
This affects seventy percent of thousands of families.

You can watch and guard for years.
Then a single battle can determine victory in a day.
Despite this, bureaucrats hold onto their salary money too
dearly.
They remain ignorant of the enemy's condition.
The result is cruel.

They are not leaders of men.
They are not servants of the state.
They are not masters of victory.

The Amazing Secrets of Using Information

This last chapter is about information, but it starts by talking about the costs of competition. It raises many of the exact same issues that are in raised chapter two. Competition is costly. Its costs take resources from the productive part of the organization. We must compete, but how do we control costs?

In this stanza, Sun Tzu extends the problem of cost in a new direction. Competition is disruptive. The changes resulting from competition put people out of work. This is even truer in economic competition where jobs are eliminated continuously.

In the realm of economics, the destructive power of competition has been called "creative destruction." It is often an evolutionary process, but as Sun Tzu points out, everything can change overnight.

Our mastery over change requires mastery and investment in the most valuable resource: information.

Creative Destruction

Competition is Destructive.
It is in the unpredictable realm of heaven.

You need a creative leader and a worthy commander.
You must move your troops to the right places to beat
others.
You must accomplish your attack and escape unharmed.
This requires foreknowledge.
You can obtain foreknowledge.
You can't get it from demons or spirits.
You can't see it from professional experience.
You can't check it with analysis.
You can only get it from other people.
You must always know the enemy's situation.

You must use five types of spies.
You need local spies.
You need inside spies.
You need double agents.
You need doomed spies.
You need surviving spies.

You need all five types of spies.
No one must discover your methods.
You will be then able to put together a true picture.
This is the commander's most valuable resource.

You need local spies.
Get them by hiring people from the countryside.

You need inside spies.
Win them by subverting government officials.

You need double agents.
Discover enemy agents and convert them.

This is one of the most important stanzas of the text. It makes two points. First, it is information and information alone that makes our decisions effective. Second, all vital information is passed from one individual to another. This is as true today, despite our computers, as it ever was. Machines can manage data, but data isn't information. The test of information is relevance. Only human beings can determine this relevance. We depend on other people for information.

The five types of "spies" are both information sources and categories of information. They are tied directly to Sun Tzu's Five Element Model, though each type is more complex than simply information about a given element.

In other words, our sources of information must complete our model, our picture of the competitive environment.

Five Spies Tied to Five Elements

Local spies are the most straightforward. They provide information about the ground, the marketplace.

Inside spies are close to decision-makers. These decisions makers can either be allies, opponents, or customers.

Double agents are our competition's information sources: suppliers, employees, and so on. They tell us about methods.

135

You need doomed spies.
Deceive professionals into being captured.
We let them know our orders.
They then take those orders to our enemy.

You need surviving spies.
Someone must return with a report.

Your job is to build a complete army.
No relations are as intimate as they are with spies.
No rewards are too generous for spies.
No work is as secret as that of spies.

If you aren't clever and wise, you can't use spies.
If you aren't fair and just, you can't use spies.
If you can't see the tiny subtleties, you won't get the truth
from spies.

Pay attention to small, trifling details!
Spies are helpful in every area.

Spies are the first to hear information, so they must not
spread it.
Spies who give your location or talk to others must be killed
along with those to whom they have talked.

"Doomed" spies are messengers. They carry our philosophy out into the competitive marketplace. This role is the most changed since Sun Tzu's time. Today, we do not send messages to mislead the opposition but also to advertise.

In the original text, surviving spies come back from the front with the latest situation. Think of this as timely information.

☐—⚹

A "complete" organization is one that is completely informed. In Sun Tzu's view, gathering this complete information is a leader's most critical role. It is also one of the best uses for our monetary resources. It must be done quietly.

Two characteristics—intelligence and fairness—out of the five qualities of a leader defined in chapter one are important to managing information. Intelligence means knowing our ground. Fairness is one of the two organizational "method" skills.

We must pay attention to the details (focus) and gather every key form of information to put together a complete picture.

We must have information sources that we can trust to keep confidences. While we can't literally kill them if they disappoint us, we must have the courage to stop dealing with them.

☐—⚹

Focus is the Basis of Knowing
We must bring together diverse facts to create a complete picture of the situation.

You may want to attack an army's position.
You may want to attack a certain fortification.
You may want to kill people in a certain place.
You must first know the guarding general.
You must know his left and right flanks.
You must know his hierarchy.
You must know the way in.
You must know where different people are stationed.
We must demand this information from our spies.

I want to know the enemy spies in order to convert new spies into my men.
You find a source of information and bribe them.
You must bring them in with you.
You must obtain them as double agents and use them as your emissaries.

Do this correctly and carefully.
You can contact both local and inside spies and obtain their support.
Do this correctly and carefully.
You create doomed spies by deceiving professionals.
You can use them to give false information.
Do this correctly and carefully.
You must have surviving spies capable of bringing you information at the right time.

Specific actions require specific knowledge. We can know generally the methods that we must use, but that general knowledge is no substitute for specific information. This is particularly true about attacks aimed at specific opponents in specific situations. We need all the details that we can get.

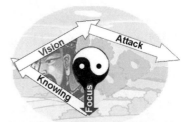

**Specific Attacks Require
Specific Knowledge**

We should think of an "enemy spy" as anyone that our opponents use as a source of information. What Sun Tzu is describing here is the best way to learn about the "best practices" in a given area. We should simply pay for it by hiring people away from our competitors. These people connect us to other valuable types of information sources.

Sun Tzu teaches, however, that building an information network must be done with extreme care. Each step in this process must be accomplished without the competition's knowledge. The more secretive we are about *our* sources of information, the less likely it is that our competition will be able to tap into them. Even messengers work more effectively if their connection to us is hidden. We must be methodical and quiet in building up and maintaining the network of people that we use as our information sources.

These are the five different types of intelligence work.
You must be certain to master them all.
You must be certain to create double agents.
You cannot afford to be too cheap in creating these double agents.

This technique created the success of ancient emperors.
This is how they held their dynasties.

You must always be careful of your success.
Learn from the past examples.

Be a smart commander and good general.
You do this by using your best and brightest people for spying.
This is how you achieve the greatest success.
This is how you meet the necessities of war.
The whole army's position and ability to move depends on these spies.

In business competition, our most valuable tool is this complete information network. In Sun Tzu's view, it is worth any price because good information can eliminate much of the other costs and waste of competition. The foundation stones of this network are information sources won from the competition.

Whenever Sun Tzu talks about history, he also means that these are methods that work better and better over time.

Basically, Sun Tzu believes that success is built over time, by moving from stepping stone to stepping stone.

In Sun Tzu's system, information management is not an ancillary task; it is the core job of a manager. This is why we assign our best people to see to it. Information is the source of all success. Information gathering can eliminate many of the most risky and costly activities of competition. All of our other skills in competition depend upon our ability to develop a solid foundation of knowledge.

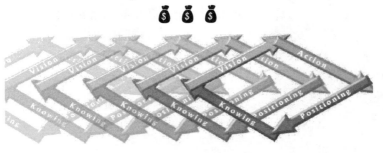

> **The Art of War is an Endless Process**
> This is the end of the book, but the competition goes
> on.

Winning Markets

The Art of War & The Art of Marketing takes Sun Tzu's lessons and helps you use them to identify markets, position against the competition, and win battles in the marketplace. You can directly apply the competitive lessons of *The Art of War* to the marketing of your company and its products. *The Art of Marketing* gives you Sun Tzu's ideas in a form that addresses the strategic issues of competition in today's terminology.

In this work, you get both books side-by-side. You get our translation of *The Art of War.* You also get Sun Tzu's ideas interpreted line-by-line to help you win the real-world battles in the marketplace.

The Art of War & The Art of Marketing deals with the external issues of winning market awareness and attracting new prospects. In many ways, it is the perfect companion book to *The Art of Sales,* which focuses on how to convert these prospects into customers. Using these books together, you can address the complete competitive process of building markets and winning customers.

The Art of War & The Art of Marketing
ISBN: 1929194021
Paperback. $14.95.

Clearbridge Publishing books may be purchased for business, for any promotional use, or for special sales. Please contact:

Clearbridge Publishing
(206) 533-9357
Fax: (206) 546-9756
Mail: PO Box 33772, Shoreline, WA 98133
E-mail: info@clearbridge.com
Internet: www.clearbridge.com

The Original Text

By far, the most complete and accurate version of *The Art of War* ever attempted. Sun Tzu wrote his original text in Chinese characters. Chinese characters have an array of possible meanings. Any English translation is only an approximation of Sun Tzu's words.

Mr. Gagliardi spent thirty years studying, using, and adapting Sun Tzu's methods before attempting this translation. He harnessed the power of the worldwide web, giving him on-line access to a variety of Chinese/English dictionaries from which to pick the right words that most accurately capture Sun Tzu's ideas. To broaden the meaning, he often uses alternate terms in the character and sentence translations to get the reader closer to Sun Tzu's original idea.

Even printing such a book is a technological challenge. Combining thousands of graphical Chinese characters with English—it would have been economically impossible to produce such a work even ten years ago. Most of Clearbridge's work explaining Sun Tzu's system would have been impossible without access to the original Chinese text.

The Art of War: In Sun Tzu's Own Words
ISBN 1929194005
Paperback. $9.95.

Clearbridge Publishing's books may be purchased for business, for any promotional use or for special sales. Please contact:

Clearbridge Publishing
(206) 533-9357
Fax: (206) 546-9756
Mail: PO Box 33772, Shoreline, WA 98133
E-mail: info@clearbridge.com
Internet: www.clearbridge.com

For Sales Professionals

The Art of War & The Art of Sales takes Sun Tzu's lessons and shows you how to specifically apply them to today's problems of contacting customers, convincing them to buy, and winning their on-going business. If you are responsible for sales or sales management, you will want this version of *The Art of War* written to address the needs of individual sales people fighting for orders from buyers. If you manage a sales force, you will want to buy this version of Sun Tzu for your people to study.

In this work, you get two books side-by-side. You get our translation of *The Art of War.* You also get Sun Tzu's ideas interpreted line-by-line to help working sales professionals in the battle for sales. If you are a sales manager or company president, you will be more than happy with the results of your sales people following Sun Tzu's advice. This is a book they will read and a philosophy they will use. The enemy is the competition. The battleground is the customer's mind. Victory is winning an on-going relationship with the customer. The two versions are shown side-by-side to give you a complete picture of using Sun Tzu's approach to modern selling.

The Art of War & The Art of Sales
ISBN: 1929194013
Paperback. $14.95.

Clearbridge Publishing books may be purchased for business, for any promotional use, or for special sales. Please contact:

Clearbridge Publishing
(206) 533-9357
Fax: (206) 546-9756
Mail:PO Box 33772, Shoreline, WA 98133
E-mail: info@clearbridge.com
Internet: www.clearbridge.com

Managing Organizations

The Art of War & The Art of Management applies Sun Tzu's techniques to building a competitive organization. A companion work to our externally focused sales and marketing versions, this book addresses the internal issues of competition: motivating your people and continually improving of your processes and products. It apples the competitive techniques of Sun Tzu to creating an externally focused organization.

In this work, you get both books side-by-side. You get our translation of *The Art of War.* You also get Sun Tzu's ideas interpreted line-by-line to help you deal with the typical problems that all managers must address.

The Art of War & The Art of Management deals with the internal issues of attracting good people, training them, and teaching them to understand the business of competition.   It also teaches managers to rethink their business processes from the viewpoint of a competitive marketplace.   It is the perfect companion book for those who want to get their internal functions in line with the external sales and marketing focus of their company.

The Art of War & The Art of Management
ISBN: 1929194056
Paperback. $14.95.

Clearbridge Publishing books may be purchased for business, for any promotional use, or for special sales. Please contact:

Clearbridge Publishing
(206) 533-9357
Fax: (206) 546-9756
Mail: PO Box 33772, Shoreline, WA 98133
E-mail: info@clearbridge.com
Internet: www.clearbridge.com

Join THE WARRIOR CLASS

The Warrior Class: 306 Competitive Lessons from The Art of War offers lessons and tests for the serious student interested in truly mastering Sun Tzu's competitive system.

The book contains over 300 lessons drawn from Sun Tzu's *The Art of War.* Each lesson focuses on a specific stanza of Sun Tzu's text. Each lesson starts with a question about competitive behavior. This question is meant as a thinking point or discussion point for those working in a study group. The lesson then quotes the text, showing how Sun Tzu would have answered that question. The page then goes on to explain Sun Tzu's thinking, using well-known examples of competitive methods from modern business.

THE WARRIOR CLASS follows the thirteen chapters in the original *Art of War.* Each chapter is introduced with its own lessons describing the focus of the chapter. There are two tests on each chapter. The first test simply checks your knowledge of the text. The second tests your understanding of the competitive issues involved in the chapter.

The Warrior Class
306 Lessons in Modern Competition
From Sun Tzu's The Art of War

by Gary Gagliardi
& Sun Tzu

The Warrior Class: 306 Competitive Lessons from The Art of War
ISBN: 1929194099
Paperback. $29.95.
Available: September, 2001

Clearbridge Publishing books may be purchased for educational, for any promotional use, or for special sales. Please contact:

Clearbridge Publishing
(206) 533-9357
Fax: (206) 546-9756
Mail: PO Box 33772, Shoreline, WA 98133
E-mail: info@clearbridge.com.
Internet: www.clearbridge.com